Also by Michael Card

The Name of the Promise Is Jesus

THE PARABLE
OF JOY

THE PARABLE OF JOY

REFLECTIONS ON THE WISDOM
OF THE BOOK OF
JOHN

MICHAEL CARD

Illustrations by Keith Mueller

A JANET THOMA BOOK

THOMAS NELSON PUBLISHERS
Nashville • Atlanta • London • Vancouver

Published in Nashville, Tennessee, by Thomas Nelson, Inc., Publishers, and distributed in Canada by Word Communications, Ltd., Richmond, British Columbia.

The Bible version used in references to the Gospel of John is the author's translation. Scripture references noted * are also the author's translation. Unless otherwise noted, other Scripture references are from THE NEW KING JAMES VERSION. Copyright © 1979, 1980, 1982, 1990, Thomas Nelson, Inc., Publishers.

Library of Congress Cataloging-in-Publication Data

Card, Michael, 1957–
    Parable of joy : the wisdom of the Gospel of John / Michael Card ; illustrations by Keith Mueller.
        p.   cm.
    ISBN 0-7852-8229-7
    1. Bible. N.T. John—Criticism, interpretation, etc. 2. Wisdom literature—Relation to John. I. Bible N.T. John. English.
Card. 1994. II. Title.
BS2615.2.C36   1995
226.5′077—dc20   95–11412
                                                           CIP

Printed in the United States of America

1 2 3 4 5 6 — 00 99 98 97 96 95

Dedicated, with profound respect, to William Lane, who nurtured the seeds of the love of Scripture in my life, who taught me a multitude of facts about the life of Jesus, but who, moreover, demonstrated in his life that the Word can indeed be fleshed out, lived, can come alive.

CONTENTS

JOHN 19

JOHN 20

JOHN 21

FOREWORD

I was both surprised and honored when I was asked to write a foreword to this book; after all, I am no great academic, no famous biblical scholar, no learned man of letters. I am merely one who has found, after years of floundering around in a miasma of ignorance and arrogance, that the answer to life's troubles and my own failings is in Christ and Christ alone, and therefore have committed my life to Him. The closer I get to Him the more interesting and demanding life becomes (when you work for the Lord, you never have time to get bored). Thus, my main criteria for assessing a book is the question, "Does this bring me closer to Christ?"

One of the problems with reading Christian books is that because they are all telling the same Truth from the same source, their authors (with some notable exceptions) fall too easily in the trap of comfortably saying the same things, often in much the same ways. To discover a new approach is a joy in itself, and Michael Card has taken a new approach in his method of imaginative analysis.

I have always found that when I sit down to read the Bible, or to devote time to prayer and worship, the minions of the World seem to unite to intrude upon my thoughts and distract my mind. Workmen will find a problem on which they need my consultation, the phone will ring with triviality after triviality, family mini-crises will suddenly emerge, and business matters will slide unbidden into my thoughts. I have learned that the powers and principalities of this world do not like me to study God's Word or books which bring me closer to the Lord. So it has been with my reading of this new book by Michael Card.

I started to read on a Saturday, and spent most of the day bouncing between the manuscript and the variety of other matters which demanded my attention. I came back to the book on Monday morning, and, safely ensconced in my study, began again to read; at once I was assailed by all sorts of distractions. Finally at about eleven o'clock, I had a brain wave. I put the book aside and for a few moments bowed my head in earnest prayer that the Lord would open my mind and heart to the book, and close it to all else according to His will. Then I began again to read. I missed lunch entirely and remained, fascinated, in the land of Judea of almost two thousand years ago, until I came to the end of the book. This, I think, the sense of being there as an eyewitness, is the great value of this work.

How often have we longed to sit amongst the crowds at Jesus' feet and listen to Him speak? How often have we longed to talk to His disciples, to watch their reactions, and hear their discussions?

Sometimes it seems as if it must have been easy for those who had the Lord right there in the flesh, present in a tangible physical way. But of course, it wasn't easy for them. In reality it was probably harder for them than it is for us. We know He is the Lord, the Christ; the Bible tells us so and great minds down through the ages have taught us so (and yet we stumble and strain at a gnat whilst we are only too ready to swallow the camel of false ideas and nonsensical "New Age" philosophies). The Lord's disciples had to face the wrath of their own priesthood and all their learned men, and it is the Gospel of John which makes it apparent how very personal such a decision was to each of them. John's Gospel is to me a very personal account, and this work brings that personality into a sharp focus.

I lack the depth of knowledge and scholarship which would enable me to project my mind into such a vivid representation of the richness of John's Gospel, but this work has brought me new insights and a sensation of feeling and texture I have not achieved before. The combination of assiduous study and imaginative extrapolation which Michael Card has brought together here is a melding of science and art. I knew that Michael was an artist, I have listened to him perform; I knew that he was a committed Christian and a biblical scholar for I have heard him speak; and yet this book surprised me, not that Michael Card should write it particularly, but that anyone should have such a sense of immediacy, of the living presence within the Gospel and the feeling of actually being there. The real excitement in studying John with the insight that this book provides is that as we achieve a closer feeling of being *there* and *then,* we also achieve a closer feeling of Him being *here* and *now.*

Douglas Gresham
Ireland, February 1995

PREFACE

⁂

From the moment I felt the call to teach the Bible, it was John's voice I heard and understood most clearly. His account of Jesus' life is unique because the relationship he had with Him on earth was unique. He was the disciple Jesus loved.

Focusing in on one book of the Bible, if properly done, does not close one off; instead it opens up the entire book of Scripture. John has led me into the Old Testament Law and the Prophetic writings, but primarily his Gospel is a door into the Wisdom writings. He presents to us Jesus, the Wisdom of God (Proverbs 8:22ff).

I began by teaching a class of elderly ladies in my home church when I was about fourteen. They were a most forgiving group. Later in college I taught as much as my class schedule allowed. These essays are the result of working through John's Gospel with all ages and types of people. Most of the insights came from others who asked the kinds of questions that interacted with the text at the level of the imagination.

At the university I came to know William Lane. He encouraged us, his students, to listen to the text of Scripture, to hear the voice of the original writers, and to understand the historical background in which they wrote. This all made the Bible come alive to my imagination. More importantly, it caused the truths of Scripture to sink deeper into the heart. It allowed a more frontal encounter with the One who is the Truth. This approach to the Bible sees Jesus not as a subject but as a Person with whom we are in relationship.

What This Book Is and Is Not

This book does not pretend to be an academic commentary. That would be beyond my simple abilities; besides, many fine commentaries already exist. While there is, I hope, a good academic basis for most of this book, it is meant to be more of an exercise of the imagination. There is much straightforward teaching in it, but the lion's share of the essays are designed to help the reader, through his or her imagination, to interact with the details John provides to help make the stories come alive.

John is a wonderful painter. He gives eyewitness details that serve no other purpose than to help us "be there" with Jesus. What other reason could there be for noting that the fragrance of the perfume filled the house where Mary anointed Jesus' feet or that Jesus constantly directed His listeners' attention to fields of wheat, the sound of the wind, fig trees, and children? John wants us to see all these things with the eyes of the heart so that we might truly understand with all our beings what Jesus was trying to communicate.

I have placed the text of the Gospel of John at the beginning of each chapter so you might study it before you start working through the essay. Try reading it to yourself out loud, for this is how all reading was done in the ancient world. I have tried to translate it as closely to the original as possible. I hope this will give you a feel for the antiquity of the text. Modern translations using our own figures of speech are wonderful and allow us to understand easily, but it is also good to keep in mind the span of time these documents have been in existence. They are ancient, and it helps to read them with this tone somewhat preserved.

As you read through the text, I ask that you be on the lookout for three things: First, watch for incidents when Jesus was misunderstood by the crowd or the disciples. You may want to mark these passages with an *M*.

Second, watch for quotations and allusions to the Wisdom writings of the Old Testament (Job, Psalms, Proverbs, and Ecclesiastes). These you can mark with a *W*.

Finally, be aware of eyewitness details that only John would have knowledge of: the time of day, words spoken only in whispers, and the sounds and smells surrounding the scene. These you might mark with a *D*.

As you move into the essays, absorb what is useful and pass over what is not. We have done our best to keep errors at a minimum, but still there are in all likelihood some mistakes. These are entirely my fault, and for them I apologize.

Realize, as you listen to the text, that you are sitting at the feet of the last living contemporary of Jesus. Give him the respect he deserves. Pay close attention as he takes you aside and whispers explanations in your ear, things he only realized years after the fact. None of the other Gospel writers will do this for you.

John's desire was not to make a name for himself; in fact, he did not even sign his work. He was not concerned about giving you more information as much as he cared that you would come to believe and know in your heart that his friend Jesus is truly the Son of God (John 20:31).

INTRODUCTION

He is the last of the disciples left alive. The community of seven churches he pastors, situated along a postal road, stands in awe of him: John the Elder. *Elder* is as much a description as a title, for he is pushing eighty hard. In a world where forty is "getting along" and sixty is ancient, eighty is miraculous. But miracles are nothing new for the son of Zebedee; his entire life has been one long miracle, at least the life he's had since he met the Nazarene.

He was a simple man from a simple place. But what happened to him was not at all simple, or was it? He was a follower, a disciple. Someone Jesus loved. Someone He trusted. With his own hands, John had touched Him. Those now-tired, old eyes had looked into the mystery of His fine, intellectual face. John had been asking himself all those years, *What did it mean? What does He mean?* The answers he came up with never seemed enough. Perhaps there was more to having the answer than knowing an answer.

Owing to his unusual age, a rumor had begun to spread. Something was up, and some believed John might go on living until the Lord returned. There was a kernel of truth to the rumor, as there often is with rumors. There was a confused version of something Jesus once said about John remaining alive until His second coming. But at this time in the history of the church, even as it is now, there was much confusion about many of the things Jesus had said and done.

What was clear, however, was that to stand in the presence of the last living disciple was to realize that he needed to commit to writing as much as he knew before his lips were silenced forever. So, to quell a rumor concerning his approaching death, to clarify some of the sayings of Jesus, to refute certain heresies, and to satisfy the members of his community who urged him to do so, John began to write. He wrote for the children in the fellowship he so dearly loved. For the fathers he sometimes pitied with tears because they could not begin to imagine all they had missed. For the young men who only had him to tell them, with his words that so often felt clumsy, like fish flopping out of a net. He wrote because they wouldn't leave him alone until he did, because He wouldn't leave him alone until he did, because he missed the sound of Jesus' voice so much sometimes he thought his heart would break. Perhaps he wrote in the hope that through the words of just one of his sentences he might hear once again the familiar sound of His voice.

The Synoptics, the "with-one-eye" Gospels of Matthew, Mark, and Luke, had already been well circulated. Everyone knew by heart the stories they contained. John set out to fill in the gaps. He thoughtfully omitted major sections so he could substitute stories that no one had ever heard, stories he'd been telling and preaching for more than sixty years.

These stories came together by themes, as good sermons do— light and darkness, wisdom and foolishness, the misunderstood Messiah. As he dipped the stylus in the ink, the words were as fresh as they had been half a century earlier, made all the more vibrant by the Spirit that breathed into him and blew like a wind. And like a wind, John sometimes didn't know where he was being blown by the story . . . or where it came from . . . or where it was taking him as he began to scratch away at the parchment.

Like any good storyteller, John waited as excitedly as his hearers to see where the stories would end up. Writing them down, working through them again in his imagination, was almost like being back on the road again with Jesus. Details came to mind that he had thought were long lost: tired feet from their long journeys, the fear of the Pharisees, the feeling of having his breath taken away by those luminous words of the Nazarene.

He remembered how again and again the people had misunderstood Jesus' words and works, and how, after He would make His most deeply spiritual pronouncements, the crowd would often completely miss His meaning. He would talk about living Water, and they would see only a well. He would speak of the Bread from heaven, and they would only want a meal. It was a major motif in

His life, a "Motif of Misunderstanding." It set Jesus apart in a lonely way sometimes. He came to His own, but they could not comprehend what God had done, was doing, in this seemingly simple Galilean.

As he remembered and wrote, John began to see the purpose of all the misunderstanding, how it set Jesus apart as the Wisdom of God over against what men called "wisdom."

And so it was to the Wisdom writings of the Old Testament he naturally turned. Each unique metaphor, every new name he called Jesus by, came from the pages of the Wisdom literature of the Old Covenant: Job, Psalms, Proverbs, Ecclesiastes. He remembered Jesus' quoting from their passages time and again. As he turned each page of the Writings, John discovered a new name, a new nuance to Jesus' life.

It was no coincidence for John that at precisely the same time he was writing his Gospel the debate was raging in the Jewish council at the city of Jamnia as to whether Psalms, Job, Ecclesiastes, Proverbs, and the Song of Solomon should be included in the Jewish biblical canon. In years of preaching and teaching he had seen again and again the exquisite connections between the Writings and the life of Jesus. John did not need to hear the decision from the council. He pronounced his own verdict by basing most of his Gospel on these writings; his major themes are all rooted in Wisdom (see the Appendix).

The essence of the depth of John's picture of Jesus is its simplicity. Light, water, bread, seed sown. Jesus is revealed through the immediate, the tangible. He left out the parables of Jesus because, for John, Jesus' entire life was a parable; a parable of misunderstanding, of pain, and of joy. He remembered as he scratched away, only occasionally pushing himself back from his table to wipe away a tear brought to the surface by a memory that came out of nowhere and forced him again, through his powerful, childlike imagination, into the very presence of the Galilean he loved and longed for and missed with all his heart.

So here they are. The words—and more than that, the thoughts and feelings of the last living contemporary disciple of Jesus. Hear them. Come sit at his feet and listen to what John has to say about this Lord of his, the Friend he leaned against at their last meal together, whom he had been leaning on ever since. The One John would have us all learn to lean on.

Notes on the Translation

The translation used in this book is remarkable only in so far that it was done by one of the world's poorest linguists. I tried to make it as verbatim as possible, and this will no doubt cause some difficulties. I retained terms like, "into the Age," instead of "eternity." Instead of "was not able" and similar phrases, I opted to try "did not have the power," which reflects the root meaning of the word *dunomis.* In the commentaries that follow my translation I have paraphrased some of the Scripture I quote, particularly dialogue, to help you see how it might have been spoken in today's language.

In Greek a question can sometimes expect a yes or no answer as indicated by a small particle. Whenever possible, I tried to reflect this, even though it does not read as smoothly and may seem a bit tiresome after a while. For example: "He will not do greater things than this, will he?"

Jesus' mysterious phrase that is variously translated, "verily, verily," or "I tell you the truth," I left in the original, "AMEN, AMEN." I chose to capitalize it, and other similar phrases, to reflect their unusual, mysterious, and unparalleled nature.

The tone of John's narrative often shifts when he begins to preach. I have blocked off these sermonic sections in *italic type.* I hope that these will allow you to better recognize the change of voice.

I have also tagged some of the repeated characteristics of John's writing. For example, in the footnotes to the Scripture (found below the double rules at the bottom of each page) I've marked with an *M* comments noting the Motif of Misunderstanding. I've marked with a *W* comments related to the Wisdom writings of the Old Testament. I've marked with a *D* John's frequent, insightful details gained from the fact that he was an eyewitness to the events he is describing, and other telltale signs that identify John as the writer of this Gospel.

THE PARABLE
OF JOY

JOHN 1

By the word of the Lord the
heavens were made.
Psalm 33:6

The Word and Deed

JOHN
1:1–2

1 *IN THE BEGINNING was the Word and Deed. And the Word/ Deed was with God and the Word/Deed was God.* **2** *He was with God IN THE BEGINNING.*

In the Old Testament, what God says He does. He speaks a word of creation and behold, creation happens. Nestled between the verbal bookends of the two "in the beginning" phrases lies the basis of John's understanding of who, at the heart of it all, Jesus is: the Word. Jesus Christ is the

---

1–2 It is important to learn to recognize the tone of one of John's sermons. This tone, evident here in the introduction, will reappear throughout the Gospel from time to time to summarize large blocks of material and prepare us to enter new sections of narrative.

solid, fleshed-out figure of what is only a shadow in the Wisdom writings.

Debar is Hebrew for "word," and it means both "word" and "deed." In the Old Testament, words accomplished something, whether it was the words of a covenant or the pronouncement of a blessing or even a curse. Thus God spoke the *Debarim* of creation, "Let Light be," and the words made the light shine and darkness roll back like a scroll.

John tells us that God has spoken a powerful word of recreation, of salvation, and so the Incarnation happens—a Word spoken and done, pronounced in syllables of flesh.

The introduction to this Gospel tells of the speaking of that Word. The remainder of the book tells of the deeds of the One who was the living Word.

Even as His children neither listened to nor understood what God first said or did, so now His living Word is not comprehended, neither what He says or does, though He is full of meaning, grace, and truth.

For John, the truth of this will be demonstrated in the parable of Jesus' life. What Jesus says will always be reflected in what He does and vice versa. He will do something like open the eyes of the blind and then speak the deep truth that He is the Light of the World. Jesus will tell His sorrowing friends that He is the Resurrection, and then that word will be validated as Lazarus comes hobbling out of the tomb. Jesus feeds five thousand and then tells us He is the Bread of Life. What He says is always validated, illustrated, fulfilled in what He does. For He is the *Debar,* the Word and Deed of the Father.

As it will be throughout his Gospel, John relies on the Wisdom writings to define his understanding of who Jesus is. It is no mistake that the opening statement of John's Gospel begins and ends with the phrase "in the beginning." This phrase, which is also the Hebrew title for Genesis, the first book of the Old Testament, is important to John. It will appear and reappear in the Gospel as well as in the letters John will later write. This phrase establishes a mood, a context, an aroma of the authority of the Old Testament. It points the direction for understanding John's central theme for explaining who Jesus is and what He means. The Word.

THE CREATOR-CHRIST

JOHN
1:3–4

³ *Through Him all things came into being and without Him nothing came to be, not one single thing.* ⁴ *In Him was* LIFE *and the* LIFE *was the* LIGHT *of all people.* 🎵

When John sought to describe his friend Jesus, two words stuck in his mind: *light* and *life*. But these were not meant to be merely theological terms, for as the source of light and life it is Jesus who is the true Creator. Every hillside He climbed had been fashioned by His own hand, even the final hill called Calvary. Every tree that offered Him coolness and shade had been carved out of nothingness by Him, even that dark tree from which the cross would be carved.

This One who was "in the beginning" was not merely standing by as the world was created; He was, in fact, the creative force of God, His Word. When God said "Let Light be," the Light that in fact already was, was Jesus. The notion that it was Christ who was the creative Person of the Trinity was a part of the church's earliest confession of Him and is contained in the Wisdom writings (see Prov. 8:22). Three separate writers in the New Testament speak of Jesus in this way. Besides John, Paul writes in Colossians 1:15–17:

---

3   In association with the "genesis" phrase that surrounds the opening statement, here John further develops the Old Testament context by associating Jesus with the Creation.

He is the image of the invisible God, the firstborn over all creation. For by Him all things were created that are in heaven and that are on earth, visible and invisible, whether thrones or dominions or principalities or powers. All things were created through Him and for Him. And He is before all things, and in Him all things [hold together].

Similarly, the writer of Hebrews [Apollos?], said:

In these last days [He has] spoken to us by His Son, whom He has appointed heir of all things, through whom also He made the worlds. (1:2)

The One who is Life and Light, who was from the beginning, is the One through whom the Father created time and space. The Creator-Christ is also the Re-Creator, the source of new creation as well as the old, the One in whom all creation is sustained and held together.

The purpose of John's sermon is to set the tone for the rest of the Gospel. The Light came to the darkness, but the darkness could not, would not, understand. The Creator came to His own, but the creatures misunderstood His coming.

Whenever John speaks of Light, the darkness is always there in the background of his story so that we might understand the brilliance of the One who is the true Light. When he speaks of the Life, a dead man will be somewhere close by. When the Wisdom of God opens His mouth as Understanding Incarnate, the foolish will always be close at hand, misunderstanding. Light and Life are the keys John uses in this great song of faith; they are the primary colors in this stunning portrait.

THE MISSING NATIVITY

JOHN
1:5

⁵ *The* LIGHT *in the darkness shone, and the darkness did not understand It.* ✇

When we speak of the nativity of Jesus of Nazareth, we invariably turn to the pages of Matthew or Luke. There we find wise men and shepherds, a stable and a star, the scenery of Christmas. Rarely if ever do we go to John's Gospel during December; its prologue, which speaks so wonderfully of the Incarnation, has largely been relegated to theological discussion and debate. There is no smell of the stable here.

"There are no birth narratives in the Gospel of John," my professors at the university would say. While I see no need to challenge that point of view, I wonder if more is going on in the prologue than selective remembering on John's part.

John has had a lifetime to look back, to ponder in his own heart all the wondrous things Jesus said and did. Mary, Jesus' mother, has been a part of his extended family for no one knows how long. She, too, had been with Him. The features of her face, her smile, her sense of humor, her gentle laugh perhaps remind John of Jesus.

---

5   The Light shines through the Word even as God's first word in creation called the Light to shine. The phrase "did not understand it" prepares us for the Motif of Misunderstanding that will pervade almost every chapter of the Gospel.

When John finally sits down to write his account, he replays all the events of the birth in his mind—which Mary has no doubt recounted to him again and again—and he goes straight to the heart of the matter. He begins by telling us about the One he calls the Word and His coming into this dark world. As he writes, two words come to the surface of John's mind: *light* and *life*.

These two concepts, attributes, qualities, are what John remembers most clearly about Him. He remembers the sound, moreover, the *tone,* of Jesus' voice as He referred to Himself by both these names. Of all that He is to John and to us, He is especially Light, and He is Life.

"In Him was Life," John wrote. Jesus was not merely alive, though He was certainly that. Mary remembers the sound of His cry. But more than that, infinitely more, life was *in* Him. Life that was more than breathing and a heartbeat; it was whatever it is that breathing and beating hearts are a result of. Life, the very thing itself, was in Him. He was Life come alive. It was in Him, so it was His to give. In fact, that is precisely why He had come.

"That Life was the Light of men," John scratches onto the parchment. He pushes himself back from the table and remembers a thousand examples of the truth of what he has just written. Remembers dark people who, after a simple word or a touch, went away with this same Light alive on their faces. Remembers how this Light first came blazing into his own personal darkness when Jesus first asked, "What do you want?" Life that was alive and that was Light. That was who He was.

There is, I believe, a birth narrative in the first chapter of John's Gospel. It is only one verse, but it says as much about Jesus as the other narratives, though it doesn't contain as much information:

The LIGHT in the darkness shone, and the darkness did not understand It.

This is John's nativity. It should be read before Matthew and Luke because it prepares us to hear them more clearly. It contains them both. The Light that is Jesus shines into, around, and above the darkness of the stable, the darkness of the world, and the deep darkness of our own hearts. But the Light is not understood, not

by the wise men or the simple shepherds or by you and me. We cannot comprehend how Light and Life can be alive in a Person. No one can. Like the wise men and the shepherds, we are left to adore and to wonder how this can be, to pray for the Life to come to life in us, to ask God to let this Person who is the Light shine in our hearts forever.

HAVING FAITH MEANS FOLLOWING

JOHN
1:6–34

6 There was a man sent from God. John was his name. **7** This one came as a witness to testify about the Light, that all might believe through him.

8 This one was not the Light but came to testify about the Light. **9** [Jesus] was the true Light which enlightens everyone who comes into the world.

10 *He was in the world and even though the world came to be through Him the world did not know Him.* **11** *To His own He came and His own did not accept Him.* **12** *But to as many who accept Him He gave the right to become children of God,* **13** *who were born not of blood, or of the will of the flesh or the will of a husband, but born of God.*

14 *And the Word/Deed became flesh and pitched a tent among us and we looked upon His glory, the glory of the Father's only Son, full of grace and truth.*

6–9   It might seem strange that John the Baptist appears so early in John's Gospel. This points to the severity of the heresy that taught that John was the Messiah. As late as A.D. 200 there were still groups who worshiped John as the Messiah. We will hear a number of times from John's own lips that he is not the Messiah but merely "a voice."

12   John will frequently summarize the plan of salvation in a single verse—in this case, "But to as many who accept Him He gave the right to become children of God." This is a major feature of one of his sermonic conclusions and the hallmark of a true preacher of the gospel.

14   The context of the opening sermon, so thoroughly rooted in the Old Testament, precludes the notion that John's central theme of the "Word"

(continued on next page)

15 John testifies about him, he cries out, saying, "This is the One of whom I said, 'The One who comes after me surpasses me because He was before me.'"

16 *Because from His fullness we have all received grace on top of grace.* **17** *The law was given through Moses but grace and truth came through Jesus Christ.* **18** *No one has ever seen God. It is the only Son of God, in the heart of the Father, who has explained Him.*

19 This is the testimony John gave to the priests and Levites sent from Jerusalem to ask him who he was. **20** He confessed and did not deny. He confessed, "I am not the Christ."

21 They asked him, "What then? Are you Elijah?"

"I am not!"

"Are you the Prophet [like Moses]?"

And he answered, "NO!"

22 Then they said to him, "Then who are you? Give us an answer to give to the ones who sent us. What do you say about yourself?"

---

might be based in the *logos* of Hellenistic philosophy. The Word as flesh is meant to combat another heresy, a form of gnosticism called Docetism, from the Greek word *dokeo,* which means "to seem." The Docetic gnostics taught that Jesus did not come in the flesh but was instead a spirit that came on the body of the Nazarene and departed before the cross.

15   Note the use of the historical present tense, "John testifies." This is a literary device that draws us into the present.

19   One testimony to the impact of John's ministry was that the Jews would have to send an official delegation all the way from Jerusalem to investigate his ministry.

20   John will insist again and again that he is not the Messiah.

21   The priests' and Levites' question is based on the prophecy in Micah 4 that Elijah would come before the Messiah. John insists that he is not this Elijah. Yet Jesus in Matthew 11 and Mark 9 will claim that John was, in fact, the Elijah who was to come. Jesus warns that this truth is only for those who can receive it. There is no conflict, as it might seem. The question of the Jews belies the notion of reincarnation. John is not Elijah returned. John has come in the spirit and power of Elijah. He has come from the place of Elijah, with the dress of Elijah, with the diet of Elijah, and with the message of Elijah.

The question, "Are you the Prophet?" reveals the priests' and Levites' basic misunderstanding of who the Prophet would be. John will make much of

(continued on next page)

23 He said "I am [only] 'a voice crying out in the wilderness, "Make straight the way of the Lord," ' as Isaiah the prophet said."

24 The ones who were sent [to investigate John] were of the Pharisees. **25** They asked him, "Why then do you anoint if you are not the Anointed nor Elijah nor the Prophet [like Moses]?"

26 John answered them, "I anoint with water, but in your midst stands One you do not comprehend. **27** He comes after me. I am not even worthy to untie the thong of His sandal."

28 (These things happened in Bethany on the other side of the Jordan where John was baptizing.)

29 On the next day he sees Jesus coming and says, "LOOK! the Lamb of God, the One who takes away the world's sin. **30** This is the One of whom I said 'After me comes a man who surpasses me because He was before me.' **31** I did not recognize Him but still came baptizing with water so that He might be revealed to Israel."

32 John testified, saying, "I saw the Spirit descending as a dove from heaven, and it remained upon Him. **33** I would not have

---

the fact that Jesus Himself is the Prophet like Moses promised in Deuteronomy 18.

23 Some have wondered if John, who went to live in the desert, might have gone to live with the Essenes. It is interesting that when asked the purpose of his ministry he would quote a verse that was basic to the Essenes, who saw themselves as the ones who were preparing for the coming of the Messiah in the desert (see 1 QS viii, from the *Manual of Discipline* found at Qumran).

24 John's baptizing presented a problem for the Pharisees since the only baptism they recognized was proselyte baptism by which a Gentile would become a Jew. But John was baptizing people who were already Jews. Later we will see an argument erupting concerning "ritual cleansing" as the Jews seek to come to terms with John's baptism of repentance.

29 "The next day" is Saturday, the Sabbath (see Isa. 53:7). Note the unusual use of present tense: "he sees." The abrupt change is supposed to catch our ear and force us into the present with John beside the Jordan. Scholars refer to it as "historical present tense." It is an ancient literary device.

32–33 John the Baptist's significant testimony reveals a truth that applies to everyone who comes to Christ. At the moment he sees the dove he seems to be saying that his entire life suddenly makes sense. It is the same for all who come to know Jesus. This is Christ-centered enlightenment.

recognized Him except the One who sent me to baptize with water said, 'Whoever you see the Spirit descending upon and remaining, this is the One who will baptize with the Holy Spirit.'

34 "So have I seen and testified . . . this is the Son of God." ❧

The opening verse of this story is abrupt, as abrupt as jumping into the cold water of the Jordan, which is where we find ourselves, wet-footed, with John the Baptist. He comes from the place of Elijah, the wilderness, wearing the clothes of Elijah, camel skin, eating the food of Elijah, locusts and honey, and bearing the message of Elijah, "Repent, for the kingdom is at hand."

John the Baptist's mother, Elizabeth, was a relative of Mary, the mother of Jesus, so the story describes two cousins meeting at the river. Our writer's mother was Salome, also a relative of Mary, so John, the writer of this Gospel, is also a cousin of Jesus. (Salome followed Jesus and the disciples along with the group known only as "the women.")

The story seems to interrupt John's beautiful sermon like an uninvited guest. What does the maniac preacher/wildman from the wilderness have to do with the luminous themes John is developing? The explanation comes from an understanding of the life situation of the Gospel John is writing.

It would be almost impossible to underestimate the popularity of John the Baptist. As late as A.D. 200 some of his followers still worshiped him as the Messiah. In Acts 19:3 we meet "believers" who still only know John's baptism. This story, told here in the beginning of John's Gospel, took place sixty years or so earlier, when John the Baptist was at the height of his popularity. But the fact remains that within the community for which this Gospel was written, groups still engaged in worshiping John the Baptist as the Messiah.

This helps us to see the sense of speaking of him so early in the narrative. Jesus has just been established as the Light. Now it is important for John's readers to hear that John the Baptist is not that Light. In fact, in a litany of denials we hear the Baptist insisting he is not the Christ or Elijah or the Prophet like Moses but only a simple voice in the wilderness.

The ministry of John the Baptist serves as an important landmark in the geography of the faith. Before John, as far back as Abraham and the other patriarchs, having faith meant waiting. The exercise of belief was almost completely a matter of waiting for the Messiah. John the Baptist was the final faithful "waiter." After John, faith is expressed by following the Messiah. This significant shift from waiting to following was immediately preceded by an act of repentance in preparation for the Coming. That is where John fits in. His baptism of repentance, which so confused the Jewish authorities, perfectly prepared the waiting faithful to become faithful followers.

The statement about the loosening of the sandal thong is all the more significant, given the Baptist's popularity. "I am not worthy even to untie His shoe," he says. The rabbis taught that "every task a slave does for his master shall a disciple do for his rabbi, except the loosening of the sandal thong." This act was seen as too demeaning a task for the disciple. Now John confesses his unworthiness to even be the slave of Jesus. The humility seen in this statement as well as in his later remark, "He must increase; I must decrease," sent a strong message to those who were still following the Baptist all those years later. John the Baptist was not the Christ or a Prophet like Moses, but was, like John and his readers, only a servant of Jesus.

That confession of unworthiness speaks of a deep humility, but deeper still was the meekness of the One who was willing to both loosen the sandals as well as wash the feet of His disciples.

THE FIRST DAY

JOHN
1:35–39

35 The next day John stood there again with two of his disciples. **36** He saw Jesus walking by and said, "LOOK! The Lamb of God!"

37 The two disciples heard what he said and followed Jesus.

38 Jesus turned around and saw them following and said, "What are you looking for?" And they said to Him, "Rabbi (which is translated 'teacher'), where are You staying?"

39 He said to them, "Come and see."

They went and saw where He was staying and spent the day with Him. (It was around 4:00 P.M.) 🦥

I t was a Sunday. Their first day together. John, the disciple, was with the Baptist, along with Andrew, beside the Jordan when Jesus passed by. Jesus said nothing. The prophet looked up and with a tone so full of hope and wonder it would be impossible to describe said, "Look!"

As John turned and saw Jesus, the Baptist whispered in amazement, "The Lamb of God." John could no more have stayed there

---

38 The disciples called Jesus "rabbi," a term Jesus would not allow everyone to address Him by. The word is based on the Hebrew *rav*, which means "great." Unless the person really seemed to understand all that this title meant, Jesus refused to allow Himself to be called "rabbi."

ᴰ**39** Notice John's remembrance of the smallest detail. This points to his being an eyewitness. He knows details that only an eyewitness would know. Look for such details in the narrative. They always have a purpose.

by the river than he could have suspended himself in the morning air. There was simply nothing else to do but follow.

"What are you looking for?" They were the first words Jesus had ever spoken to him. His voice was flat, surprisingly normal, but sincere. Jesus had a northern accent, a drawl, that might have been embarrassing to some northerners because generally, people tended to think it made them sound ignorant. As John writes these first words, alone in his room, he starts and looks around. It is as if he heard them spoken over his shoulder, "What do you want?"

After all, how do you answer such a question from the Messiah? "What do I want? What am I looking for? The world, eternal life, a place beside You in the Kingdom, to be reborn, to never lose hope again, to be whole . . ." John might have asked for anything, but his simplicity, his embarrassment, his nerves perhaps, made him stutter only, "Where are You staying?" It was a question that meant more than even John knew then. He was not merely asking to see Jesus' domicile; in his heart he was asking to see a home.

Jesus' house belonged to someone else. It was a place of poverty, even by John's standards, but it was clean and full of air and light.

They sat down together, the three of them—Jesus, Andrew, and John—around a low, bare table. This first meeting was where it all began for John. Later he remembered every word Jesus said, every expression that passed across His face, every story, every word of banter between them. Excited, as all new friends are at finding one another, they shared a secret joy as they realized they would become lifelong companions. Before any of them realized it, the day had passed. Through the small window they could see that it was getting dark outside. Andrew and John stood up, stiff at having sat in one position for so long. They were embarrassed at how difficult it was to say good-bye, though they had just met Jesus a few hours ago. They walked out into the dusk. The excitement they both felt seemed to fill the air around them; they were numb with it and filled with it. And this was only their first day.

A New Name

JOHN
1:40–42

40 It was Andrew, Simon Peter's brother, one of the two who had heard John and followed, **41** who went out first and found his brother. He said to him, "We have found the Messiah!" (which is translated "Christ").

42 He led him to Jesus. Having looked at him, Jesus said, "You are Simon, the son of John. I will call you Cephas" (which is translated "Peter"). ✳

Andrew walked home in the fading evening light, his heart bursting with excitement, joy, relief. He thought to himself, *I must tell Simon.*

Simon, like Andrew, was a fisherman and a good one at that, more because of stubbornness than skill. When everyone else had called it a night, Simon would stay out until he had something to show for his labor.

He, too, was a simple man; what you saw, you got. But unlike gentle Andrew, Simon's simplicity made him run hot or cold. His joy could sometimes bruise a rib; his anger, an eye. Simon was the first to laugh at a joke (even if he didn't completely get it), the first to cry at a wedding, and the last to hold a grudge.

---

41   In Andrew's actions we see the beginning of evangelization. Andrew tells Simon. One person tells another. This is still the most fruitful form of evangelization. Note that whenever a Hebrew term is used, such as "Messiah," John will translate it into Greek for his readers.

When Andrew found him, he was at the dock loading his nets into the boat. Andrew expected some opposition, but instead, without a word, Simon walked off toward town. Andrew followed in silence. At first Simon walked, but soon he was running; Simon's bulk, however, made it easy for Andrew to keep up with him. They reached Jesus' house out of breath.

It was as if He knew they were coming. Jesus had lighted a lamp and was standing outside the door. It was this image of Him that Andrew most vividly remembered years later when persecution came: Jesus standing in the dark doorway with a lighted lamp in His left hand, smiling, waiting for Peter to come to Him.

He looked at Simon—no, He *stared* at him the way someone stares at a work of art or a sunset, bemused. "You are Simon, John's son," he said. He wasn't asking; He was telling. "You will be called Cephas." The tone of His voice was as matter-of-fact as if He had said, "We will be having fish for supper."

It wasn't as if Jesus was giving Simon a new name but simply speaking for the first time the name he should have had all along. Cephas recognized himself in that name. Even as it was said of Adam, "Whatever Adam called each living creature, that was its name," so what Jesus called Simon was his name. It perfectly described who he was—the rock, lumbering, stubborn, dense, obstinate—but also solid, sure, stable, and above all, strong.

Cephas. It was not a common Aramaic name but its Greek equivalent, *Petros,* was; so eventually that's what everyone started calling him. Jesus would give nicknames again. "James and John, the sons of thunder," He would say with a sad twinkle in His eye.

Once, sitting by the fire, He spoke of the future, something He rarely did. He told them about a time when the Father would hand each of them a white stone with their own new names written there (see Rev. 2:17). The disciples began asking Him to tell them what their new names would be because they could sense Jesus already knew what they were. But He would say nothing. Later, after the subject had changed, He looked across the fire at Cephas, smiling as if to say, "I couldn't wait to tell you yours."

JACOB'S DREAM COMES TRUE

JOHN
1:43–51

43 On the next day He decided to go into Galilee. Jesus found Philip and said to him, "Follow Me."

44 Now Philip was from Bethsaida, the city of Andrew and Peter. **45** He then found Nathanael and said to him, "He who Moses wrote about in the law! and also the prophets! We have found Him . . . Jesus, the son of Joseph from Nazareth."

46 And Nathanael said to him, "Can anything good come out of Nazareth?"

"Come and see," Philip said.

47 Jesus saw Nathanael coming toward Him and said, "Look, a genuine Israelite, in whom there is no guile."

48 Nathanael said to Him, "How do You know me?"

"Before Philip called you, I saw you under the fig tree," Jesus answered.

49 "RABBI!" Nathanael answered, "You are the Son of God. You are KING of Israel!"

50 Jesus answered and said to him, "Because I told you I saw you under the fig tree, you believe? You will see greater things."

---

43   Note that on Monday Jesus purposefully decides to go to Galilee and look for Philip.

44   Philip was from Bethsaida, although, like the rest of the disciples, he seems to be living in Capernaum now.

18

⁵¹ [Jesus] said to him, "AMEN, AMEN! I say to you, you will see heaven open and the angels of God ascending and descending on the Son of Man." ❧

As Andrew ran to tell Simon, so Philip ran to tell Nathanael. In the end of John 1 there is a lot of action and many pictures of telling the good news.

There is no word concerning Philip's relationship to Nathanael, or Bartholomew, as he is called in other Gospels.

Maybe they were cousins, perhaps simply friends. When the Twelve are sent out two by two, Philip and Nathanael are always grouped together. They are a team.

You can hear the excitement in the broken phrases Philip uses to tell Nathanael about Jesus: "He who Moses wrote about. . . . We have found Him!" he says. He is speaking to someone who is a student of the Scriptures. "He who Moses wrote about" is a reference to an individual described in Deuteronomy 18:15 as the "Prophet like [Moses]." In Jesus' day there was confusion among the people concerning who this Prophet would be. Some saw him as a precursor to the Messiah. Others identified him as one and the same with the Anointed One. Clearly, this prophetic figure will become central to John's presentation of Jesus.

In Nathanael, we come face to face with our first real skeptic. "Nazareth!" he whines. "Can anything good come out of Nazareth?"

His response is not as unwarranted as it might seem. The town of Nazareth, where Jesus was from, was situated in Galilee, a province on the fringes of the promised land. This area was referred to scathingly as "Galilee of the Gentiles" because, among other reasons, as many as seven pagan deities were worshiped in the province. It was therefore looked upon with disgust by proper Judean Jews. Galilee was second only to Samaria in ill repute. How could anything promising come from such a polluted place?

Philip knows Nathanael well enough not to argue. Instead he issues the invitation that is the heart of all true evangelism: "Come and see."

As Nathanael approaches Jesus, the wheels are set in motion for a unique encounter. Before they actually meet, Jesus speaks a compliment, almost a blessing, to the stranger. Nathanael is caught off guard by His words, words full of grace in contrast to Nathanael's earlier negative reference to Jesus and His hometown.

"Behold, a true Israelite," Jesus says. (Nathanael's earlier words, "Can anything good come out of Nazareth?" implied that Jesus was not a true son of Israel.)

At the moment, nothing would seem further from the truth than Jesus' next statement about Nathanael: "In him there is no guile." But Jesus is able to see deeper than the surface. He doesn't need testimony about anyone in order to fully know him or her.

Nathanael's tone sounds a bit uneasy. "How do You know me?"

Jesus knows him to the extent that it makes him uncomfortable, but His answer could not seem more ordinary. "I saw you under the fig tree."

What happens next is remarkable, though it is rarely seen as being so. In a flash the skeptic becomes a saint. Jesus' seemingly mundane response sets off nothing less than an explosion of faith: "Rabbi, You are the Son of God. You are King of Israel!"

What could have possibly happened inside Nathanael's heart and mind to result in such a dramatic change? Here is where background and an understanding of life situation is vital.

The key to unlocking the mystery is Jesus' reference to the fig tree, which had symbolic significance in Israel as a sign of the nation. But Jesus' words have more than symbolic meaning. The fig tree was a common place for prayer, especially for young rabbinic students, which Nathanael may well have been. If he was specifically under a fig tree when Philip called him, chances are he was in prayer. This is an interesting fact, but it still does not fully explain the drama of the story. "So what?" we might say. "His prayers were interrupted. After all, he did seem a bit irritated at first."

The final piece of the puzzle involves first-century rabbis' teaching about prayer. The Jewish believer was taught that "he who, when he prays, does not pray for the coming of the Messiah, has not prayed at all." With the rise of the pharisaic movement, basically a "back-to-the-Bible" group, the hope for the coming of Christ had been reawakened. It was on everyone's mind and in everyone's prayers.

Thus, if Nathanael had been at prayer, chances are he was praying for the Messiah. Perhaps this is why Jesus refers to him as a true Israelite; his faith was focused on waiting for the Coming. When Jesus tells Nathanael He saw him under the fig tree the implication is (and it is just an implication) that Nathanael put two and two together in his mind. Only one person could have known, could have heard his solitary prayer for the Messiah: *the Messiah Himself!* As the pieces fall together in his heart and mind Nathanael finds himself on his knees. The true Israelite declares Jesus is the King.

Jesus seems almost as surprised by Nathanael's response as we do. He says, in essence, "You believe because of this? You shall all see greater things than this."

Jesus' earlier reference to "guile" sets up a comparison that only becomes evident here. Nathanael is the guileless Israelite. By contrast, Jacob, who was known as the "man of guile" in the Old Testament, is the trickster, the cheat. If nothing further were said in reference to him, the mention of guile would not have the force it does. But here Jesus returns to Jacob. He speaks a prophetic word that perfectly ties the story together. Jesus begins to talk about Himself in terms of Jacob's dream (see Gen. 28). Jesus, the Son of Man, will be the One upon whom the angels of God ascend and descend. The ladder in the legendary dream of the man of guile is in fact a Person. Jesus' discreet return to the topic of Jacob calls us back to His description of Nathanael as the "guileless one." What Jesus is saying to Nathanael and the disciples—and to us—is that what Jacob could only dream about, a Way to heaven, has become a reality. Jesus is Jacob's dream come true!

JOHN 2

THE ZEAL FOR YOUR HOUSE WILL
DEVOUR ME.
PSALM 69:9*

PREOCCUPIED
WITH PARTIES

JOHN
2:1–11

¹ On the third day there was a wedding feast in Cana of Galilee. Jesus' mother was there. ² And both Jesus and His disciples were invited to the wedding feast.

³ When the wine was gone, Jesus' mother said to Him, "They do not have wine."

⁴ "What is that between you and Me, My dear? My hour has not come yet," Jesus said to her.

⁵ "Whatever He tells you, do," His mother said to the servants.

---

1 The third day is Tuesday.
4 Whenever Jesus makes this statement—"My hour has not come yet"—it is implied that a time is coming for Jesus.

6 Now there were six stone water jars there, used by the Jews for purification, each measuring about 30 gallons.

7 Jesus said to them, "Fill the water jars with water."

And they filled them to the top.

8 Then He said to them, "Draw it out now and bring it to the master of ceremonies."

And they brought it.

9 The master of ceremonies tasted the water that had become wine but he did not know where it had come from, but the servants who had drawn the water, they knew.

The master of ceremonies called the bridegroom and **10** said to him, "Everyone else sets the expensive wine out first and when they are drunk he breaks out the cheap stuff. You have kept the good wine till now."

11 This was the beginning of signs performed by Jesus in Cana of Galilee. And He manifested His glory. And His disciples believed in Him. ✇

Once, on a mission for a friend, I was sent to the highlands of Scotland. In the course of fulfilling my task, I stayed with a wonderful family who, though I was a complete stranger, treated me as an honored guest and prepared a special dinner for the occasion. Each of us was given a single large baked potato, one leaf of lettuce, and a sizable glass of cold water. This was our feast, not because the food was exotic but because normally the family would divide one of these big potatoes amongst everyone. It was an eye-opening evening for me.

Many of us have lost the mentality of feasting. For us, every meal is a feast. We eat until it hurts and then stop, or perhaps eat just a bit more and wonder why our weight is a problem. We do not know what it is like to truly feast because we do not know what it is like to be hungry.

Jesus and His disciples knew the excitement of anticipating a feast. In fact, whenever He was not preaching or teaching, you would most likely find Jesus at a party, a banquet, a feast, or some kind of get-together. It could be said that He was preoccupied with parties. What seemed to annoy the Pharisees most was not that

Jesus went to so many parties, but that He seemed to enjoy Himself so much. Perhaps that is the real reason they called Him a winebibber. He was just having too much fun.

The feast, or party, is part of the foundation of Christianity. Here at Cana, Jesus performs His first miracle, so it could be said that our faith, in a sense, began at a party. Early in the history of the church times of fellowship resembled parties or love feasts. "See how much they love one another!" the unbelievers said as they witnessed the get-togethers of the first followers of Jesus. The quality of their new lives in Christ overflowed in their feasts. How could a group of Christians coming together not resemble a celebration? Even as the Christian faith began at a banquet, so it will come to completion at a wedding feast.

An ancient tradition says this narrative is an account of the apostle John's own wedding feast. He shows intimate knowledge of what went on by revealing what is whispered in the ear of the bridegroom. Perhaps it was he. Mary, his aunt, seems to feel some kind of special responsibility and concern that the party goes well. Who knows? It is consistent with his personality that John would not tell us it was his wedding since he does not even mention his own name in the course of his Gospel!

John gives us the detail that it is the third day, always a symbolic day in his Gospel, the day of life over death and light over darkness. Jesus and His disciples are there. When the wine is gone, Mary informs her son.

Jesus responds, "What is that between you and Me, My dear?" or perhaps, "Why should we get involved?"

I have yet to hear a satisfactory explanation for Jesus' reluctance, but something in the gentle tone of His voice tells Mary that He still intends to do something about the situation. She informs the servants to do whatever He tells them to do.

The stone water jars are only partially full. This is probably because the guests have used some of the water for the ceremonial cleansing of their hands when they arrived. The jars need to be filled back up.

If we multiply the size of the jars by their number we come up with about 180 gallons of water (or wine). One of my bright students once calculated that this amounts to nine hundred fifths of wine, which, at an average cost of thirty dollars a bottle, amounts to twenty-seven thousand dollars' worth of wine!

What is most striking about the miracle is the fact that it seems to strike almost no one as miraculous. There is no pronouncement from Jesus, no waving of the hands, only the benign request to fill up the jars and take a pitcher over to the master of ceremonies. The subdued tone of the miracle serves to set it in stark contrast to the final wedding feast of the Lamb.

Through this subdued, almost reluctant, demonstration of His power, it is said that Jesus manifested His glory and became the very object of their belief. This value system, which says simple is better than complex, humility is better than ostentation, is characteristic of John's picture of Jesus.

The toastmaster, who would tell jokes and keep the party atmosphere going, tasted the "water that had been changed into wine." He realized that something out of the ordinary had taken place, not the miracle of the transformation, but rather a departure from customary etiquette. (We are not told if he ever learned of the miracle. Only the servants seem to be privy to what happened, and servants usually know how to keep their mouths shut.)

"Everyone serves the expensive wine out first and waits till the guests are drunk. Then they bring out the cheap stuff," he says. "But you have saved the best for now."

Sometimes this phrase is quoted, "You have saved the best till last." I have heard sermons based on this translation. The literal translation says more, however. God does not save the best till last; He saves the best for *now,* for the sacrament of this present moment. The only question is, will we respond to His extravagant invitation to join Him in the banquet of the moment? He holds nothing back for later. We are the ones who hold back and offer our lame excuses for not coming to His party of the present. His gracious invitation is the way He manifests His glory.

With 180 gallons of excellent wine at their disposal, one wonders how long the wedding feast at Cana went on! What is certain is that when those privileged guests went home they knew they had been to a party. They had feasted no doubt as much on the presence of Jesus as on the food and wine.

That first rural celebration, the subdued, almost secret miracle, is recorded by John to allow us to anticipate a banquet that had made the prophets' mouths water hundreds of years before. When at last it does take place, Jesus will feast with His bride at the wedding supper of the Lamb (see Rev. 19). John, the beloved, was given the privilege of dining with Jesus at Cana, of leaning against Him at the Last Supper, and finally of attending in the Spirit that final feast where God had prepared a banquet of aged wine (Isa. 25:6). We need to recapture the mentality of feasting, and John gives us a place, called Cana, to start.

FIGHTING ON BEHALF OF THE POOR

JOHN
2:12–22

12 After this He went down to Capernaum with His mother and brothers and disciples. But they did not stay there many days. **13** And the Passover of the Jews was near. So Jesus went up to Jerusalem and found **14** in the Temple the ones selling cattle and sheep and doves, as well as the coin dealers . . . just sitting there.

15 He made a whip out of small cords and threw everyone out of the temple, along with all the sheep and cattle. He poured

---

12   Capernaum seems to have been the base of operations for Jesus' ministry.

14   It is important to have in mind specifically where this area of the temple was. This was known as the "court of the Gentiles"; it was as close as "god-fearing" Gentiles could approach the temple. (God-fearers were Gentiles who wanted to worship in the temple but who were unwilling to submit to circumcision thereby becoming full proselytes.)

The Jews demonstrated their contempt for the Gentiles by moving the marketplace, which before was always held on the Mount of Olives, into the temple complex itself. This in fact may have been the first time it had appeared there. There is no reference of its being there before A.D. 30. This would help explain Jesus' surprise and indignation at seeing it here for the first time. I speculate that after this event the market might have been moved back to the Mount of Olives. The next year, A.D. 33, Jesus finds it set up again in the Temple and for a second time drives the merchants out.

Destroying the marketplace was a very pharisaic thing for Jesus to do. The market belonged to Annas, a powerful Sadducee. Jesus was disrupting an important source of the Sadducees' income. This might have been His first step toward the cross.

out the coins of the moneychangers and overturned the tables. **16** To the dove sellers He said, "Take these things from here. Do not make My Father's house a house of merchandising."

17 His disciples remembered that it had been written,

"The zeal for Your house will devour me."

18 The Jews said to Him, "What sign do You show us for doing these things?"

19 Jesus answered and said, "Destroy this sanctuary and in three days I will raise it."

20 Then the Jews said to Him, "It took forty-six years to build this sanctuary and You, in three days, will raise it?"

21 But the sanctuary He was speaking about was His body. **22** So when He was raised from the dead His disciples remembered that He had said this and they believed the Writings and the Word of Jesus. 🕱

Y ou will not find the first expulsion from the temple in the other Gospels. It is only here, in John. He knew his readers were aware of the fact that Jesus' last public act before His crucifixion was the tearing up of the marketplace in the Gentile court; that episode was described in the Synoptics. What John wrote about was an earlier, separate incident when the traders were also expelled from the temple by the Nazarene. This was Jesus' first public act; thus His public ministry was bookended by a literal fight for prayer and the poor.

After spending some time with His family in Capernaum, Jesus headed to Jerusalem for Passover. Matthew called Capernaum "His own town." It was the closest thing to a home He ever had

---

17   It is important to note that the disciples of Jesus remember this incident in light of Psalm 69:9, a passage from the Wisdom writings. This points to John's continuing use of these writings.

ᴹ**20**   Here we see the Motif of Misunderstanding. The Jews are only partly right. The temple was not finished even then. It was begun in the eighteenth year of Herod's reign and wasn't completed until A.D. 64, only six years before it would be destroyed.

after being thrown out of Nazareth. This time spent with His family and disciples represents the calm before the storm.

We know Jesus went to Jerusalem at least once as a twelve-year-old boy. It is safe to assume that He had been there for other Passovers as well, if not every one. But this year something is different.

Coming into town, Jesus notices that the marketplace for the temple is not on the Mount of Olives, where it has always been located. As He comes close to the temple, He hears an unaccustomed noise. He enters the outer court, the court of the Gentiles, and discovers the reason for the cacophony. Annas, one of the high priests, has moved his marketplace into the very temple itself!

Jesus does not explode all at once. He finds some small cords and ties a knot in one end to make a whip. This act shows premeditation. Among the groups He attacks, the moneychangers and the cattle and sheep dealers, Jesus specifically turns on the sellers of sacrificial doves or pigeons. This detail is vital to understanding the story. John has given us this specific information for a reason.

Jesus singles out the dove dealers because the dove was the sacrifice of the poor. Provision was made in the Law for the sacrifice of a pigeon to replace normal lamb or cattle sacrifice so that the poor would not be cut off from worship at the temple. In fact, Joseph and Mary offered a dove for Jesus as an infant, to redeem their firstborn son.

Earlier, when the marketplace was outside the temple, a dove sacrifice cost about four cents. Now, inside the temple, the price was seventy-five cents! Part of Jesus' indignation was that the poor were being cut off from sacrificing to their God.

The second temple expulsion, as described in the Synoptics, includes two passages from the Prophets to explain Jesus' scandalous actions. It is important to notice that in John's account of this first expulsion, a passage from the Wisdom writings gives shape and meaning to the event. Jesus' disciples remember the words of Psalm 69: "Zeal for Your house will devour me."* As he will throughout the Gospel, John bases his account on the Wisdom writings. It is touching to realize that this psalm also speaks prophetically of Jesus' being offered vinegar to drink (see v. 21). This act of Jesus will bring together the forces that will ultimately arrest and crucify Him. It is important that it is remembered in the words of a crucifixion psalm.

After the ruckus is over, as the merchants gather up bleating sheep and scattered coins looking sideways at Jesus, muttering under their breaths, the Jews ask for an explanation. Note that Jesus is not condemned for what He did. Everyone knows His actions were right (in fact the Pharisees in particular would have applauded Jesus' attack on a Saducean institution like the temple market); the only question is one of authority. "Who gave you the authority to do this?" they ask.

In John's Gospel, Jesus will rarely answer questions. This situation is no exception. He gives no explanation precisely because He alone has the authority and owes no one an explanation. Instead Jesus prophesies.

This is our first major example of the Motif of Misunderstanding (M), one of the distinctive motifs in John's Gospel.

"Destroy this sanctuary," Jesus says, "and in three days I will raise it."

It would be difficult to underestimate the attachment the Jews had to the temple. They called it *ha makom,* "the Place." In this place they met with God, in this place they offered sacrifices for their sins, in this place their entire culture was secured. When the temple was later destroyed—razed to the ground with not one stone left standing on another—the character of Judaism radically changed.

As almost always happens in religion, what was initially intended to be a reverence for God degenerated into a love affair with a building. Jesus' scandalous words, "Destroy this sanctuary and in three days I will raise it," would stay lodged in the Pharisees' minds for years. Those words would be the basis for charges against Him two years later. And years after that, His disciples, specifically Stephen, would be persecuted and martyred for following the One who spoke against the temple (see Acts 6:14).

The structure of the Motif of Misunderstanding is virtually always the same:

a. Jesus will make a deeply spiritual pronouncement.

b. The next verse will indicate that the people grossly misunderstood what He meant. Their misunderstanding will go beyond a mere failure to grasp His intention. They will always completely misinterpret what He has said.

Keep a close watch for the occurrence of this motif. It has a cumulative effect.

"It has taken forty-six years to build this temple," they say. In fact the temple was still under construction and would not be completed for another thirty-four years. It would then be destroyed only six years later by Titus.

"But the sanctuary He was speaking about was His body."

Here is John's unique, backward-looking perspective. Only John will pull us aside and whisper in our ear an explanation that only became clear years later.

The aside goes on to say that after everything happened, just as Jesus had said it would, the disciples would remember that even in His early ministry Jesus had said that He would rise from the dead.

A MAN NAMED NICODEMUS

JOHN
2:23—3:13

23 While He was in Jerusalem during the Passover feast, many trusted in His name, seeing the signs He was doing. **24** But Jesus would not trust Himself to them, because He knew them all and because **25** He had no need for testimony about them. He knew what was in a person.

---

23   This is the first reference to "the signs He was doing." Note that it appears in a negative context associated with people to whom Jesus will not entrust Himself. Throughout the Gospel, Jesus will seek followers who are willing to believe without seeing, that is, followers with true faith. Those who demand miraculous signs will be seen, not as unable to come to faith, but as impeded by their demand to see first before believing.

25   This statement prepares us to meet Nicodemus in John 3. The Gospel was not originally written with chapter and verse divisions, so 2:23 might have been a better place to begin chapter 3.

3:1 Now there was a Pharisee named Nicodemus, a leader among the Jews. **2** He came to Him during the night and said, "Rabbi, we know that You are a teacher, come from God, for no one could do these signs You do unless God were with him."

3 Jesus answered, "AMEN, AMEN, I say to you, unless a man is reborn, he is powerless to see God's kingdom."

4 "How can a man be born who is already old? He cannot enter the mother's womb a second time!"

5 "AMEN, AMEN, I say to you," Jesus said. "Unless a man is born of water and Spirit he is powerless to enter God's kingdom. **6** What is born of flesh is flesh. What is born of spirit is spirit. **7** Don't stand there gaping because I told you to be re-

---

1 Nicodemus comes almost certainly as a result of the first temple expulsion. This is the same Nicodemus who will help prepare the body of Jesus in John 19:39.

2 Nicodemus acknowledges that Jesus is a "teacher, come from God." Jesus will say that the Pharisee is "Israel's teacher." This is an important distinction. Nicodemus will represent Israel's wisdom; Jesus will represent the wisdom of God. But note that the basis for Nicodemus's statement is the "signs" Jesus is doing. In the next chapter Jesus will remark that the people will only believe on the basis of what they see. He desires followers who will believe without seeing. The term *signs* will almost always appear in a negative context in John's Gospel.

3 Faith should stand alone, rooted in the mystery of the new birth. The Kingdom is not achieved by personal righteousness but by an act that God Himself makes possible. It represents a change in a person's life that is so radical it can only be called "new birth." This new birth:

1. Makes us new persons.
2. Gives us the ability to enter heaven.
3. Gives us sonship or daughterhood with God.
4. Is our birth into eternal life.

"New birth" was a rabbinic term applied exclusively to Jewish proselytes. It signified that through baptism they had become completely different persons. The rabbis even debated whether a man who was born again as a proselyte could marry his own mother since he was a "new person."

M4 The motif of misunderstanding is seen here as Jesus says something deeply spiritual and the immediate response of the hearer is blatant misunderstanding based on an inability to see beyond the physical.

born. **8** The Spirit/wind blows where it wishes; you hear the sound of it but you do not know where it comes from and when it goes away. This is how it is with anyone who is Spirit-born."

9 Nicodemus answered, "How can such things be possible?"

10 "You are Israel's teacher," Jesus said, "and you do not know about these things? **11** AMEN, AMEN, I say to you, what I know I say, and what I see I testify about. But you do not receive My testimony. **12** If you do not believe the earthly things I spoke of tell Me how will you believe if I speak to you about heavenly things?"

13 *No one has ever ascended into heaven except the One who descended out of heaven, the Son of Man.* ❧

T
he wind had been blowing fiercely all evening. It was already late when the old man knocked softly on what he hoped was the right door. He was nervous, ready to bolt at the slightest sign that the Nazarene would not be willing to receive him. After all, Nicodemus had seen a vivid display of His terrific temper earlier that morning in the temple, although it had gratified the old Pharisee to see the market of the Sadducees lying scattered all over the temple court in shambles.

In one sense, he was coming out of gratitude to Jesus for having the courage to finally do something that should have been done long ago. It was good to see a young man of true zeal in

---

8   Again Jesus makes an example lesson using a wonderful play on words. The same word in Greek, *pneuma*, signifies both "wind" and "spirit." The same is true of the Hebrew word for both, *ruach*.

10   The Old Testament speaks of the radical change of the new birth (Ezek. 36:26). Nicodemus would have been well aware of these passages. The only excuse for his failure to understand is that it had never happened to him.

"Israel's teacher" is a technical term for a Pharisee. Nicodemus, like Israel, connected faith to signs while Jesus posits instead the idea of the new birth. Faith is rooted in personal experience with the Spirit: The new birth isn't something we do but something God does.

13   Whenever Jesus speaks of the ascending/descending motif in this Gospel, the term "Son of Man" is present. (The motif also appears in Proverbs 30:4.)

Israel, another Phineas. In another sense, Nicodemus came out of curiosity, hoping to see a miraculous sign. He had only heard the rumors about the wonders the Carpenter could do.

Finally, he came to seek clarification for the Sanhedrin. The delegation that Nicodemus earlier had had a hand in sending to investigate John the Baptist had come back with more questions than answers. Why should he be baptizing Jews? Wasn't baptizing only for Gentile proselytes? The council needed to know. All these questions, mixed with a thousand hopes, churned inside the elderly statesman as he stood in the dark outside the door.

He was startled by the sound of the latch opening. It was the right place, for there stood the Nazarene, a welcoming expression on His face. The passion Nicodemus had seen earlier in the temple court had drained from His dark eyes. He looked smaller somehow, standing alone in the middle of the room.

"Rabbi," Nicodemus said, "we know that You are a teacher, come from God, for no one could do these signs You do unless God were with him." Nicodemus was uneasy, and he always spoke louder when he was nervous. He sounded insincere even to himself.

Jesus did not respond right away. In fact, Nicodemus was taking a breath to speak again when Jesus finally said, "AMEN, AMEN, I say to you, unless a man is reborn, he is powerless to see God's kingdom." Jesus said these words with a strange solemnity that contrasted with the warmth with which He had first greeted Nicodemus.

The Pharisee felt as if the theological discussion might begin now. He countered with a question that was formulated to force Jesus to clarify what He had just said: "How can a man be born who is already old? He cannot enter the mother's womb a second time!" The problem was that Nicodemus had been so nervous waiting for Jesus to speak that once Jesus opened His mouth Nicodemus became so caught up in formulating his own response that he really didn't listen to what the Nazarene was saying.

Jesus was speaking of the same radical change Ezekiel had prophesied (Ezek. 36:26). Nicodemus, who knew his Bible backward and forward, should not have misunderstood. As the question was leaving his lips, he was embarrassed at having said it.

"You must be born of water and Spirit," Jesus said, now smiling. Nicodemus thought the reference had been to the waters of physical birth; after all, he had just posed the ridiculous prospect of entering the womb a second time. But Jesus was once again speaking from Ezekiel and the reference to the clean water in which God promised to wash His people (36:25). Jesus and John the Baptist had been baptizing on the authority of this passage. It explained their actions at the Jordan.

"You should not be surprised," Jesus said, almost scoldingly. "Does not the Spirit/wind *(rauch)* blow wherever it wishes?" He said as the shutters blew open. "Hear it? But you don't know where it comes from or when it leaves. This is how it is with all who are born of the Rauch of God."

The old rabbi was clearly out of his depth. He mistook the rushing sound of the blood in his ears for the wind Jesus was talking about.

"How is this possible?" he muttered to himself as much as to Jesus.

"I'm only telling you what I've seen and heard," Jesus said, perhaps a bit frustrated now. He might have said, "Why can't you people understand? I'm talking about earthly things, of water and wind, of birth, things that surround you every day. Still you do not, will not, accept it. How would it be if I spoke to you about the things I've seen in heaven?"

He was intense but not irritated. He was not cutting Nicodemus off but inviting him into the discussion, leaving the old rabbi space to make the realization on his own.

Jesus spoke as if the refusal of the people to hear was wounding Him. It had been a long time since Nicodemus had heard someone speak of spiritual matters with such passion, and it frightened him. He had only come to talk theology, not to have the rug pulled out from under his religious world. For Nicodemus and his council associates, religion was a matter of doing, of keeping the Law, of being good. But Jesus seemed to think that true religion was based on something God was doing, giving birth to new sons and daughters by His Spirit.

Jesus had been looking toward the open window. Now He turned back and faced the confused old man. The expression He wore spoke peace in spite of obvious pain and passion. Nicodemus did not feel he was being excluded because he did not understand, although that was the common practice of his own group. Instead Jesus was extending His hand.

They said their *shaloms,* but Nicodemus knew it was not good-bye. He would see Jesus again. As he made his way back through the dark streets toward home, he felt the joy he had first known as a young student of the Scriptures.

"I must look again at the passage in Ezekiel," he said out loud to himself. It was not with self-condemnation but with forward-looking joy that he thought, *The only reason I've not understood it is because it has never happened to me! Perhaps I should give up asking to see miracles and ask God instead to make me a miracle.* As he turned the corner the wind whipped around the side of a building and knocked him on his back. Nicodemus sat in the dark and laughed like a schoolboy.

THE SERPENT IN
THE WILDERNESS

JOHN
3:14–15

14 *As Moses lifted up the snake in the desert, so it is necessary for the Son of Man to be lifted up,* **15** *that everyone who believes in Him may have life eternal.* ❧

The children of Israel had seen more than enough miraculous signs since their exodus from Egypt. They were literally eating miracles every day in the form of the manna that came from heaven. But the food for which they had begged was now detestable to them. So the Lord sent snakes into the camp, venomous serpents. Their poisonous bite would cause a terrible burning pain, so they became known as "fiery serpents." Naturally a cry went up from the camp. "We have sinned!" the people said to Moses. "Ask the Lord to take the snakes away!"

When the tired, old prophet asked God what to do, a bizarre answer was given to him. Instead of simply making the plague

---

14 "Lifted up" is always used in the Gospels as a metaphor for crucifixion. In our time, however, the phrase has become associated primarily with praise; consequently, some people have misinterpreted this saying of Jesus (along with His words in John 12:32) to mean that if we praise Jesus this will "draw all peoples" to Him. This is not the intent of Jesus' saying. Certainly praise is one of the central keys to being a follower of Christ, but our praise is not what draws men and women to Him. Instead it is His perfect sacrifice and provision for our sin. This draws us to Him. Our response is then praise.

disappear, as He would normally do, God asked for a sign from the people, a sign of faith.

He instructed Moses to make a brass snake and fix it to a pole. "Tell the Israelites," God said, "that everyone who will look toward the serpent will be healed." So Moses made an image of the very thing that was causing their suffering and demanded that the people look up to it before they could be made whole again. Looking at the symbol of their suffering became the cure for the suffering itself (Numbers 21:4–9).

Jesus (or perhaps John, for it is not clear who is speaking here) uses this remarkable and otherwise obscure story to explain His destiny and purpose on earth. Even as the brass serpent was "lifted up" so that all could see, so Jesus will be lifted up—will be crucified. Like the serpent in the wilderness, all who look in faith toward that cross will find healing from the serpent's fiery sting.

The brass serpent was a model, an "incarnation," of the Israelites' pain and suffering; it was an image of their sin of not trusting God, of calling His provision detestable. Even so, as Jesus suffered for our sin, His "lifted-up" cross became an icon for our suffering as well as His. As difficult as it must have been for the Israelites to look in faith toward an image that embodied their pain, so it is painful—but vital—for us to look intently at the suffering symbol of the cross if we are to find healing.

There is an interesting postscript to the story of the brass serpent. Years later the children of Israel gave the object a name, "Nehushtan," and began to worship it with incense. What had formerly been intended as a focus for their faith in God became instead an object of idolatrous worship. The story of how Hezekiah destroyed the idol is in 2 Kings 18.

We shake our heads at those foolish, unbelieving Israelites, but the same tendency exists in us today. Many of us make the cross into an idol (or even worse, a fashion accessory!). Some see it as an end instead of as the means for God's provision of salvation to the world. The subtle transformation from icon (an object that helps us properly focus our faith) to idol (an object of worship) can sometimes happen almost imperceptibly. Our faithfulness in not losing sight of the suffering it represents allows us to keep the cross in perspective.

JOHN'S SERMON AND SUMMARY

JOHN
3:16–21

16 *This is how God showed His love to the world. He gave His one and only Son, that everyone who believes in Him may not perish but have life eternal.* **17** *For God did not send the Son into the world to pass judgment on the world, but to save the world through Him.*

18 *Anyone who believes in Him is not judged, but the unbeliever has already been judged by his failure to believe in the name of God's only Son.*

19 *This is the judgment . . . Light has come into the world. But everyone loved darkness rather than the Light. And why? Because their works were evil.* **20** *For everyone who does evil hates the Light, will not come to the Light, because the Light exposes their works.*

21 *But the ones who do the truth come to the Light to show that what they have done has, in truth, been done in God.* 🎔

At the close of this first major section of narrative, John gives one of his most famous sermons. In red-letter editions of the New Testament, it is often printed as the words of Jesus. A closer look (and an ear for the tone of the words) reveals that it is probably John who is speaking once again,

---

16–20 Serving as John's sermonic conclusion, this closing block of material refers back to the prologue and ties together all the threads of thought. This sums up everything through the talk on the new birth. Note again the capsulated statement of the plan of salvation at the conclusion of the sermon.

summing up the major themes he has used thus far, looking back to the opening sermon, and introducing new themes that will follow.

One of the hallmarks of John's short sermons is that they almost always contain the plan of salvation in a single verse. Here it is verse 16: "This is how God showed His love to the world. He gave His one and only Son, that everyone who believes in Him may not perish but have life eternal." In perhaps the most beautiful words ever written, this verse presents the *why* as well as the *how* of God's redeeming love. Later, in his letters, John will betray a preoccupation with the question "What is the meaning of love?" Here he gives himself and all of us the answer.

In the King James Version the sermon reads almost like a song: "for God so loved the world . . ." God caused Him to be lifted up like the serpent in the wilderness, becoming sin for us on the cross. He did not condemn the world; He would save the world by His being lifted up.

Even as in the Old Testament, where all it took was the glance of faith, now all God requires is that we should believe this unbelievably good news.

In verse 19 John sums up, by means of a verdict, the theme of Light he introduced in the first verses of chapter 1. As the Light and darkness were divided "in the beginning" by the Word of God, so now the coming into the world of the Light of the World has divided those who love the Light from those who embrace the darkness.

THE FRIEND OF
THE BRIDEGROOM

JOHN
3:22–36

22 After these things Jesus and His disciples came into Judean country. He was staying there, baptizing. **23** And so was John, in Aenon, near Salim, because there were many pools of water there. And the people were coming and being baptized.

24 (John had not been thrown into prison yet.)

25 Some of John's disciples were discussing ritual washing with a Jewish person. **26** They came to John and asked, "Rabbi, the One who was with you on the other side of the Jordan, the One you testified about, just look! He christens and everyone is coming to Him."

27 John answered, "A man cannot receive anything unless it

---

22   "After these things" serves as a loose chronological connection.

23   Note that they are baptizing there simply because there is a lot of water in that area. The earliest teaching of the church on baptism says that if there is much water one should immerse, if there is little water one should sprinkle, and if there is no water one should use sand! There were no hang-ups as to form.

24   Note that John assumes his readers know the details of the story of John's arrest.

25   It is interesting that at the site of baptism an argument arises concerning "ritual washing." The Jews are obviously trying to reconcile John's "baptism of repentance" with their own understanding of Gentile proselyte baptism. And yet here was John, baptizing Jews. Naturally they would begin a discussion of ceremonial cleansing, trying to understand John's actions.

27   We would all do well to learn this lesson.

is given to Him from heaven. **28** You heard me say, 'I am not the Christ, but the one sent before Him.'

29 "The One with the bride is the Bridegroom. But the soshben, the one who stands and hears Him, leaves with great joy because of the sound of the Bridegroom's voice. This joy is mine and has been made full. **30** It is necessary for Him to increase, but for me, to decrease."

31 *The One from above is over all. The one of the earth is of the earth and speaks of the earth. The One who comes from heaven is over all.* **32** *What He sees and hears, He testifies about and no one receives His testimony.*

33 *The one who receives it certifies that God is true.* **34** *The One God sent speaks the words of God. He gives the Spirit without measure.*

35 *The Father loves the Son and into His hands has given everything.*

36 *Whoever believes in the Son has life eternal. But whoever disobeys the Son will not see life. God's wrath remains on them.* ❧

Frrom across the village the sound of the wedding feast can still be heard, though it has begun to die down. Hours ago he escorted her from the wedding banquet; the revelers hardly noticed she was gone. He now stands guard outside the bridal chamber, for in these days brides are still sometimes stolen. He is the best friend of the bridegroom, the one above all others he can trust with his own bride. He is called the *soshben*.

He waits as the party dies down and finally comes to an end. As the soshben hears the footsteps and voices leaving the wedding feast his excitement begins to build; soon his best friend will come

---

28 Again we hear from the mouth of the Baptist that he is not the Messiah. This is yet another part of the polemic against the current heresy that taught that John was the Messiah.

29 The *soshben* is a technical term for the best man.

31–36 This is another sermonic conclusion. The opening of the sermon could be seen as a farewell to John the Baptist. He will not appear again in the narrative. The closing of the sermon speaks of the giving of the Spirit, which prepares us for the story of the Samaritan woman.

to consummate the marriage. The bridegroom will at last make his beloved his own.

As friends they have talked about it since they were boys. The soshben remembers the first time he met her, remembers the excitement of his best friend whispering to him the good news that he had found his bride. He was the first to know.

That was so many months ago, and now, at last, the wedding has occurred. A new life for his friend, perhaps even children!

As he stands in the pitch black, these thoughts bounce around in his head; his heart is full of joy for the new couple. He shares their happiness as no one else can.

At long last he hears footsteps coming down the narrow street. They seem familiar yet still it is his mission to be sure. A dark figure walks directly toward him. The soshben stiffens; it might be an impostor.

"It's me!" the bridegroom whispers. "I'm here."

He would know the voice of his friend anywhere. At last he has come. The bride is ready. The soshben steps aside to open the door to the bridal chamber. His job is done.

The dim light that comes from the lamp within the chamber illumines his friend's features. There is joy, there is relief, there is passion, and above all, there is love. As the bridegroom steps past his guardian friend their eyes meet. They are moist.

"Thank you, my friend," the bridegroom says. "There is no one I trust more than you."

The stipulation of custom says that the soshben is now to "go away rejoicing." But he needs no encouragement from custom. His task is done. His joy full.

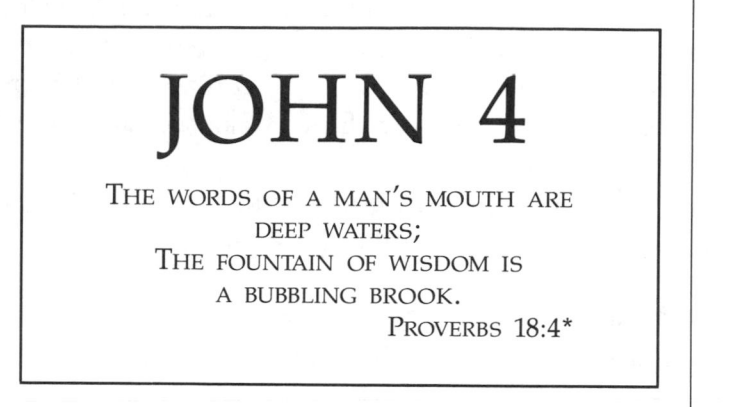

JOHN 4

THE WORDS OF A MAN'S MOUTH ARE
DEEP WATERS;
THE FOUNTAIN OF WISDOM IS
A BUBBLING BROOK.

PROVERBS 18:4*

WISDOM'S FOUNTAIN BY THE WELL

JOHN
4:1–42

1 When Jesus found out that the Pharisees had heard that He was baptizing more disciples than John **2** (although it wasn't Jesus who did the actual baptizing but His disciples) **3** He left Judea and went again to Galilee.

1–3 It seems that in order to avoid controversy Jesus leaves Judea and heads for Galilee. This provides the context for the story since Samaria lies between Judea and Galilee. In verse 2, John tells us that Jesus did not baptize. More precisely, the Greek indicates that it was not His custom to baptize. This may have been one way to avoid appearing as another "Baptist." Paul also attempted to separate himself from the ministry of baptizing (see 1 Cor. 1:14).

4 It was necessary for Him to go through Samaria. **5** He came therefore into a city called Sychar close by the parcel of land which Jacob gave to his son Joseph. **6** Jacob's well was there.

Jesus had become weary from His journey and around noon was sitting at the well.

7 When a Samaritan woman came to draw water Jesus said, "Give Me a drink." **8** (His disciples had gone into the city to buy food.)

9 The woman said, "How can you, a Jew, ask for a drink from me, a Samaritan woman?" (For Jews do not use dishes Samaritans have used.)

---

4 Some have said Jesus showed unusual compassion for the Samaritans by breaking with Jewish tradition and passing through Samaria. Yet the historian Josephus suggested that it was the custom of the Galileans, who were despised almost as much as the Samaritans, to go through Samaria (see Josephus, *Antiquities of the Jews,* XX 118).

6 Jacob's well is still there at the fork of the road to Scythopolis and Nablus. This is an historical spot. Jacob gave this plot of ground to his son Joseph (see Gen. 29), and Joseph's bones are buried there (see Gen. 33). The covenant was renewed there after the Promised Land was taken (see Josh. 24:32). Now, as Jesus speaks to the Samaritan woman, history is about to be made there again.

7 It may be helpful to have some background for the Jewish/Samaritan schism: In 720 B.C. Assyria invaded the northern kingdom and resettled the area with foreigners, who intermarried with the few remaining Jews. When the exiles of the southern kingdom returned they hated the "squatters" (see Ezek. 4 and 2 Kings 17:6–24).

ᴰ**8** John has intimate knowledge of the event. The writer of this Gospel was with the other disciples in town buying food.

9 The fact that Jesus would speak to a woman in public would have been as surprising as His speaking to a Samaritan. Rabbis did not do this. One rabbi had said, "The daughters of the Samaritans are menstruants from the cradle" (considered perpetually unclean). There was even a group of Pharisees known as the "bruised and bleeding ones," a name derived from the fact that when they even saw a woman they would close their eyes and so would sometimes run into doorways! These Pharisees taught that to even look at a woman was a sin, believing, "Each time a man talks to a woman he causes evil to himself and in the end inherits Gehinnom." Jesus later defined looking at a woman with adultery in the heart as a sin.

(continued on next page)

¹⁰ Jesus answered her by saying, "If you only knew the gift of God and who it is that is telling you, 'give Me a drink,' you would have asked Him and He would have given you the water of life."

¹¹ The woman said, "Sir, you haven't even got a bucket and the well is deep. From where then will You get this water of life? ¹² You aren't greater than our father Jacob, are You? He gave us this well and drank from it himself with his sons and his cattle."

¹³ Jesus answered her saying, "Everyone who drinks this water will thirst again. ¹⁴ But whoever drinks of the water that I will give, that person will never thirst for all time. You see the water I will give will become [not a deep well but] a fountain leaping up into life eternal."

¹⁵ "Give me this water," the woman said, "so that I won't thirst or have to come back here to draw."

I opt for the translation, "Jews do not use dishes Samaritans have used" because Jesus is asking to use her bucket. She will point out the fact that He has nothing to draw with.

10   To put this verse in its proper perspective consider Jeremiah 2:13: "For My people have committed two evils: They have forsaken Me, the fountain of living waters, and hewn themselves cisterns—broken cisterns that can hold no water." (See also Prov. 18:4 and Ps. 36:9.)

ᴹ**11**   The Motif of Misunderstanding appears here. Jesus has opened the door of the kingdom to the woman, regardless of the fact that she is a Samaritan, and she completely misses the point. Jesus' reference to the living Water might have also been difficult for her since the Samaritans accepted only the Torah and all references to living Water are found in the Prophets.

12   Note that the woman claims Jacob as her own ancestor. She feels every right to do so since the Samaritans, before the exile, were part of an unbroken line that extended to the patriarch.

13   A "Better Than" Motif appears here. See also John 6:58, which says, "Whoever feeds on this Bread . . . will . . . not die like the fathers who ate the manna."

14   One wonders if Jesus refers to the springing fountain of the Spirit in contrast to the well He is sitting beside. He often makes reference to an immediate physical object. Note also that Jesus never says, "I am the living Water." Instead He always says He is the source of the living Water.

ᴹ**15**   Again the Motif of Misunderstanding is reiterated. All the woman sees is a tired Jew, not the exalted Revealer of Samaritan legend (see the note for v. 25).

51

16 "All right," Jesus said. "Go and call your husband and then come back."

17 The woman answered, "I do not have a husband."

"What you said was right," Jesus said. "You really don't have a husband, **18** for you've had five and the one you have now is not your husband as well. You spoke the truth after all."

19 "I can see You are a prophet, Sir," she said. **20** "Our fathers worshiped on this mountain but You would say that Jerusalem is the only place to worship."

21 "Believe Me, woman," Jesus said, "an hour is coming when you will worship the Father neither on this mountain nor in Jerusalem. **22** You worship something you do not know. We worship what we do know because salvation is from the Jews. **23** But the hour is coming and now is here when the true worshipers will worship the Father in Spirit and Truth. **24** For it is certain that the Father is seeking such people who must worship in Spirit and Truth."

25 The woman said, "I know the Messiah is coming, the One called Christ. When He comes He will reveal everything to us."

26 Jesus said, "I AM . . . the One speaking to you."

27 Finally His disciples came back and were amazed that He was speaking to a woman. However no one said, "What are You seeking and why are You speaking with her?"

---

16 As with Nicodemus, Jesus engages the woman unexpectedly.

20 Like Nicodemus, the woman responds with religious talk; she speaks of institutionalized worship. Earlier Jesus had been talking about thirst. Worship is really a matter of thirst. Her reference to "this mountain" is to Mount Gerizim, where the Samaritans built a rival temple after their help was refused by the Jews in rebuilding the temple in Jerusalem in 450 B.C. (see Ezek. 4).

22 Jesus is referring to the fact that five other pagan deities were worshiped in Samaria besides Yahweh.

23 The Spirit is not bound to one place. Truth is not limited to one group or people. True worship encounters God everywhere.

25 Her response is authentically Samaritan because the Samaritans called the Messiah *Tahav,* meaning "the Revealer."

27 Note the disciples are surprised to find Jesus, their Rabbi, talking to a woman. They have learned, however, not to ask why.

28 Therefore she left her water pot and went into the city and said to the people, **29** "Come, see a man who told me all the things I ever did. Could this One be the Christ?"

30 So they came out of the city and were making their way toward Him.

31 Meanwhile His disciples were saying, "Rabbi, eat!"

32 But He said, "I have food to eat which you do not know about."

33 So the disciples started saying to one another, "No one brought Him anything to eat, did they?"

34 Jesus said, "My food is doing the will of the One who sent Me that I might complete His work. **35** There is an old saying, 'Relax, there are four months yet until the harvest comes.'

"Look, I say, lift up your eyes and see that the fields are ripe for harvest. **36** The reaper is already receiving his wages and gathers fruit into life eternal. So that the sower may rejoice together with the reaper. **37** For the word is true that says, 'One is sowing and another is reaping.' **38** I sent you to reap something which you have not worked on. Others have done the work and you have entered into their labor."

---

28   John remembers the detail that she left her jar behind. This is an eyewitness detail.

32   Jesus refers to the satisfying experience He has just had with the woman. He is speaking spiritually.

ᴹ33   Notice the appearance of the Motif of Misunderstanding. Jesus has said something deeply spiritual, and the disciples misunderstand completely.

35   Jesus quotes an ancient proverb that taught not to hurry. He says instead that it is urgent to start working for the harvest. They are in Sychar, the only area in Palestine with fields of grain. The rest of the area is too rocky, another example of Jesus' pointing to some immediate object to make his point.

36   Jesus speaks of an incredible occurrence. The image is from Amos 9:13, which speaks of a time when the reaper will overtake the sower. Throughout the Bible the coming of the kingdom is called the harvest.

37   Note Jesus makes use again of a popular saying.

38   We live and act upon an eternally large foundation laid by countless other men and women of faith.

39 Many of the Samaritans of that city believed in Him because of the word of the woman who testified, "He told me everything I ever did."

40 When the Samaritans came to Him, they asked Him to stay with them. And so He stayed two days. **41** Many more believed because of His word. **42** To the woman they said, "We no longer believe because of what you said; we have heard for ourselves. We know that this One is the true Savior of the world." 🌿

Noon was a suspicious time of day for a lone woman to be coming to the well. The cooler morning hours were reserved for carrying water, and this was a task which the women of the town always did together. So why was she there in the first place?

He was tired. His feet were tired. His back was tired. And there was an emotional weariness as well that was weighing Him down that day.

"Some water, please?"

The only thing more unusual than a woman alone at the well in the middle of the day was the sight of a Jewish rabbi speaking to a Samaritan and asking to drink from her water jar. Any self-respecting Jew would not consider even touching the water bucket of a Samaritan.

The Jews and Samaritans had been feuding for centuries. When the Jews returned from the Exile, the "half-breeds" who had inter-married with those left behind after the Dispersion were there wait-ing, wanting to help with the reconstruction of the temple and the wall. But if the years of exile had taught the Jews anything it was that keeping separate was the only way for the people of Israel to survive. The Samaritans' offer of help was refused, and the feuding and hatred began.

Racial hatred is a bizarre sort of blindness. Individuals, regard-

---

39 By contrast the Synoptics show Jesus being rejected by the Samari-tans. John wants to show that there was at least one incident when He was accepted there.

less of their personal qualities, are lumped together and labeled "worthless," "lazy," "deceitful." It is amazing that even the Jews, themselves the object of racial hatred from almost every other group on earth, would embrace such hatred of another race. It is a congenital flaw in all of us.

The Samaritan woman was put off, but not completely it seems. She entered into a discussion with the rabbi, puzzled that He should want to drink from her water jar. Most Jews avoided being touched by even the shadow of a Samaritan. He asks for so little and yet is ready to offer her everything.

"If only you knew who is asking you for a drink," Jesus says. "If only you knew . . ." John seems to be saying the same thing to every reader of his Gospel: If only you knew who this Man is.

"If only you knew," Jesus says. Then He offers her the water that is alive, the Spirit, from the depth of His heart. Jesus is not trying to be obscure. In fact He seeks to connect with her by using the objects close at hand. "You are here at a deep well," He says. "What if a fountain came to life inside your heart, leaping with the very Spirit of God? And all I ask is a drink, a cup of water."

Could it be that this incident was on His mind years later when He promised a blessing to all those who would offer a cold cup of water in His name?

"You do not even have a bucket," she says impatiently, as if to write Him off. The flat, gray, narrow reasoning of the world comes crashing down against the deep, rainbow-colored wisdom of God. He asks for little and gets nothing. Though He is the thirsty One, still it is He who offers to meet her need.

"If you drink this water you'll be thirsty in a few hours, but if you will only drink in the water I'm offering you'll never be thirsty again, not for the ages to come," says the still-thirsty Jesus.

At last the door opens a crack. "Give me this water," she says, still not knowing what she's asking for. Her tone doesn't seem completely sincere, and yet it is not completely mocking either.

"Then go get your husband," Jesus says.

She wonders to herself, *Perhaps He knows why I'm here alone in the middle of the day. Maybe someone's told Him about the rumors, most of which are true. Is His question an innocent one, or is He laying a trap?*

She offers the benign response, "I have no husband."

Whether or not she meant it to be truthful, the woman has answered truthfully and this amuses Jesus.

"You're so right," He says. The fact is the woman has had five husbands when even the most liberal rabbi says the limit is three. But note the absence of condemnation in Jesus' voice. There is no name-calling. She is not disqualified to receive the living Water.

As gently as a doctor unwraps a wound to examine it, Jesus takes the cover off her life. The wounds are deep; there were five slashes of woundedness, and even now there is an ongoing injury because she lives with a man whose love cannot embrace her as his wife.

She is discovered—uncovered—and the only thing to do is throw sand in Jesus' eyes and hope to get away. Religious talk is the grittiest, most irritating talk she knows. "You disqualify me by saying Jerusalem is the only place to find God," she says, throwing verbal sand in His face. But His concern is relentless.

"It is not your mountain or Jerusalem that's the point," Jesus says. "It is a matter of Spirit and Truth. That alone pleases God. Not My Jewishness nor your mountain. God loves people who are true, the ones in whom His Spirit, the water I'm offering you, is able to bubble up and flow through."

Her life has been laid bare, and yet she has been accepted. She has tried to escape, but arms of acceptance hold her fast. There is only one more test. The Samaritans had a different name for the Messiah. It was *Tahav*, "the Revealer."

"I know when the Messiah comes He will reveal everything to us," she whispers to the One who has just revealed everything to her.

"I AM," He says, looking down into her eyes.

It seems that all Jesus' witnesses are questionable. The shepherds who came to worship Him in the stable were disqualified by society from giving testimony in a court, as were women in general. And now His first missionary to the Samaritans is a woman whose word was about as valuable to the people as her empty bucket. It is an expression of His foolish wisdom, His unlikely strength, that He chooses unlikely men and women to tell His unlikely, unbelievable story. So how could it be that they still come running by the millions to hear Him?

The Man with the Crooked Hat

John
4:43–54

43 After those two days He went to Galilee. **44** (Jesus had testified once that a prophet does not have honor in his own country.)

45 But when He came into Galilee, the Galileans received Him because they had seen all the things He did in Jerusalem during the feast because they also went to the feast.

46 He came back to Cana of Galilee, where He had made the water wine. And there was an officer of the king whose son was ill in Capernaum.

47 When this man had heard that Jesus had come from Judea into Galilee he came and asked Jesus if He would come down and cure his son because he was about to die.

48 Jesus said, "Unless you see signs and wonders you will never believe."

49 The officer of the king said, "Sir, just come down before my child dies!"

50 Jesus said to him, "Go, your son lives."

---

44   The Synoptics introduce this saying when Jesus is rejected by His own people. John uses it when He is accepted.

46   It is incredible to imagine a king's official running twenty miles to beg a favor of a Galilean preacher.

50   The man believed Jesus' word to him, so he left. Ask yourself, What does it mean to take Jesus at His Word?

The man believed Jesus' word to him and so he left. **51** While he was going back home his slaves met him and told him his child was alive. **52** So he asked them at what time he became better. And they told him, "Yesterday at about one o'clock his fever left him."

53 The father realized that it was the same hour in which Jesus had said, "Your son lives."

He believed and all his household. **54** This was a second sign Jesus did having come from Judea into Galilee. ✠

H e had run twenty miles, had run in all his finery, his necklaces trailing behind him, his crown-like hat cocked sideways. He is a *basilikos,* a royal official. We do not know his name.

He is a desperate man, unashamed to beg a favor from a hick Galilean because, who knows? Maybe what he's heard is true and his son, his beloved son, might be healed.

"Signs are all you people are interested in," Jesus says. The kind of faith He desires is faith without seeing. But, after all, the man has run all this way. He stands there, feeling ridiculous and out of breath. Besides, it is his son he is begging for, not himself, and Jesus has a weakness for anyone who is about to lose a son.

No hocus-pocus, no arms in the air, only, "You may go, he will live." It is as if Jesus wants the miracle to be as unmiraculous as possible.

Perhaps the greatest miracle is not the healing itself. None of us is amazed at Jesus' power to heal over a distance of twenty or twenty million miles. Perhaps the great miracle is what John meant when he said, "The man took Jesus at His word."

Earlier he had said that the man who accepts the testimony of Jesus has certified that God is truthful, that what God says is true. And so the man with the crooked hat demonstrates to the whole crowd that God can be trusted after all and if He says "Go home; your son will live," then you can take Him at His word.

The slaves have come to tell him news he already knows.

"Your son will live after all," they say.

"Tell me, was it around one o'clock that he got better?" the official asks.

Their gasps are the only answer he needs. *So, it is true,* he thinks to himself.

The official comes back to his important looking house with his slaves following at a respectful distance. His son is waiting at the door. He had left, not knowing if he would ever see the boy alive again. It was desperation and hope that drove him from Capernaum to find the Galilean. He tells his wife. He tells his other children. He tells his other servants, and they tell their children. By nightfall the house is different. They have all come to believe in this Jesus of Nazareth. It is a fact they might best keep quiet for the time. But how could someone keep something like that a secret? Capernaum overflows with the news of Jesus, the city's adopted son.

A MAN
OF EXCUSES

JOHN
5:1–18

1 After these things there was a feast of the Jews. And so Jesus went up to Jerusalem. **2** There in Jerusalem, at the Sheepgate, is a pool. In Hebrew it is called Bethesda. There are five porches around it. **3** A multitude of sick people were lying here blind, lame, and withered.

---

1 This feast provides a reason for Jesus to come back from Galilee. Note John's concern for the feast days.

2 The Greek word translated "pool" denotes a large pool for swimming. This pool is mentioned in the copper scroll found at Qumran. Today it is known as the Pool of Saint Anne.

4 This comment appears to be a scribal comment or explanation that was at some point incorporated into the text. It does not appear in older manuscripts. The verse is not included in this translation.

5 There was a man there who had been sick thirty-eight years. **6** Jesus saw him lying there and knew that he had been this way for a long time.

He said to him, "Do you want to become well?"

7 The sick man answered, "Sir, I do not have anyone to cast me into the pool when the water is stirred. When I try someone else goes down before me."

8 "Rise, take your mat, and walk," Jesus said.

9 Instantly the man was well and took his mat and began walking about. And that day was a Sabbath.

10 Because of this the Jews said to the man who had been healed, "It is the Sabbath, so it is unlawful for you to carry your mat."

11 But he answered, "The One who made me well, He said to me, 'Take up your mat and walk.'"

12 They asked him, "Who is this man, this One who told you to take up your mat and walk?"

13 But the man who had been healed did not know who it was for Jesus had slipped out through the crowd.

14 After this Jesus found him in the temple and told him, "Look, you are well. Stop sinning or else something worse might happen to you."

---

6   Jesus' question may seem a strange one to ask an invalid. The response of the man shows just how insightful that question was.

9   This was an undeniable sign of the coming of the Messiah (see Isa. 35:6 and Jer. 31:8ff). Whenever we hear John say that Jesus has done something on the Sabbath we should perceive a shudder in the listening crowd. This invariably means trouble for Jesus. Again, the remarkable miracle will be overlooked simply for the sake of theological exactitude.

10   The Jews are not quoting Scripture but rather a passage from the Mishna, a collection of teachings of the rabbis from 200 B.C. to A.D. 200 in which various classes of work are outlined (Mishna Shabbth 7:2/39).

13   It has been said that Jesus did not have the power to heal anyone unless the person had faith in Him. Here Jesus heals someone who is a total stranger, and even after He has healed this strange little man, the former invalid does not know who helped him. Jesus will later heal the blind man who does not know who He is until after the fact.

14   Jesus appeals to the man on his own level. Something worse than being an invalid for thirty-eight years awaits him if he will not repent. The

(continued on next page)

15 Then the man went away and reported to the Jews that Jesus was the One who made him well. **16** Because of this the Jews persecuted Jesus, because He was doing these things on the Sabbath.

17 But Jesus answered them, "My Father is working now and so I am working too."

18 Because of this the Jews sought all the more to kill Jesus because not only was He breaking the Sabbath but He was saying God was His own Father, making Himself equal with God. �֍

What a heartless and insensitive thing to ask an invalid, "Do you want to get well?"

It was a ridiculous question, but it was, in fact, the perfect question.

The invalid's excuses were as lame as his bony legs. "There's no one to help me into the pool. . . . Someone gets in ahead of me." Jesus' question, "Do you want to get well?" points to the fact that the lack of strength in the man's body was nothing compared to the weakness of his will. Thankfully Jesus doesn't say, as He often does, "Your faith has healed you." If that had been the case the man would have been left there another thirty-eight years!

There is no sermon, no show; only the command, "Get up!" And of all the things the sick man might have said or done, of all the excuses he might have made, there was such power in Jesus' words, nothing was left to do but get up.

---

example of the man of excuses is a terrible lesson. Here is one who met the Son, felt His power, was even healed by Him, and yet betrays Him. Truly this man is the other Judas of the Scriptures.

16 The reason for persecution was because the healing was done on the Sabbath.

17 Jesus' repeated use of the word *work* is meant to goad the Jews. "My Father is working now" implies that He is also working on the Sabbath. The work the Father gave Him to do is for the Sabbath as well. The rabbinic tradition said, "God still does two works on the Sabbath: He creates and He judges."

18 Their response demonstrates that Jesus' previous statement was openly defiant.

What is most amazing about this miracle is not the man's walking again (though by that act the prophecy that the lame would walk was fulfilled); what is most unbelievable, puzzling, even disturbing, is that the healing was incomplete. The heart of the man Jesus left untouched. As he walked away, it seemed his soul was just as crippled as it was when we first saw him sitting like a sack of potatoes by the pool.

How do we know this?

Look at the end of the story.

The Jews see the former invalid walking around with his bedroll, which normally would not have caught their attention, except that this was the Sabbath, and the oral law forbade the carrying of any burden. They see no miracle, only the infraction of a rule; just as in a later passage of John, what astounds them about the man born blind is not his healed eyes but the illegal mud on his face. Their question is every bit as revealing as Jesus' first query. Not "Who healed you?," but "Who told you to pick that up?"

The man had no idea who it was. And the whining excuse he now gives the Jews is in harmony with the excuses he first gave Jesus, who had slipped away in the crowd.

As Jesus had sought out the man of excuses at the beginning of the story, so now He searches again in the crowd and "finds" him in the temple. Was he still begging? Had he returned to the pool? John lets us down at this point. We are free to assume that the man is not out testifying concerning the One who had healed him. It is at least a possibility that he was up to his old tricks because the first thing Jesus says upon finding him is, "Stop sinning or you'll wind up in worse shape than you were before."

But what could possibly be worse than being an invalid for thirty-eight years?

Then comes the last, ominous chord of the song that comprises this story, the final slap in the face to Jesus and all who love Him. "The man went and told the Jews it was Jesus who had made him well."

We hiss and groan as we watch this villain. If only we could get our hands on that sniveling little insect of a man we would . . . Well, we can. Take your hands and put them around your own neck because the man in this story is you. The one who betrays Him in the garden with a kiss is you, too, and me.

The story of the man of excuses is a lived-out parable of the sin of ingratitude. His disability makes visible a disability we all bear. We see him sitting by the vast swimming pool of healing, whining to the very Healer Himself that there's no one to help him. He clings to his disability like a lifesaver because it saves him from life itself. Excuses pour from his lips like the water pouring into the pool. And it is only by the overpowering command, the sheer brute force of grace, that he gets up and walks and breaks the rules. He has tasted the power of healing in his life but hardly knows the Healer. And that is where so many of us remain today. It is not necessarily a bad place, but it is a starting place, a beginning. If you find yourself standing on good legs with your sleeping bag under your arm, go now on your healed limbs and find Him; find out about Him.

But whatever you do, don't betray Him to the very people who would crucify Him all over again if they could—the rule keepers, the blind guides. Don't go back sniveling the name of Someone you'll never really know. "Stop sinning or else something worse might happen to you" and me.

THE PROPHET LIKE MOSES

JOHN
5:19–47

19 Jesus answered them and said, "AMEN, AMEN, I say to you, the Son does not have the power to do anything except what He sees the Father doing. **20** For what the Father does the Son is likewise doing. For the Father tenderly loves the Son and shows everything He does to Him. He will show Him greater works than these so that you may be amazed. **21** For even as the Father raises the dead and makes them alive, so the Son brings to life whoever He wants.

22 "The Father judges no one, but the judgment of all things He has given to the Son **23** so that everyone will honor the Son as they honor the Father. Whoever does not honor the Son does not honor the Father who sent Him.

24 "AMEN, AMEN, I say to you, the person who hears My word and believes the One who sent Me has life eternal and does not come into judgment but has moved out of death into the life.

25 "AMEN, AMEN, I say to you, an hour is coming and now

This is the first long discourse in John's Gospel.

20   Many maintain a rigid distinction between the various Greek words for love, saying that *agape* is always used for the highest form. This distinction may not be so rigid. Here Jesus uses the word *phileo,* which some claim is a lesser form of love; yet Jesus uses it of the Father's love for Him.

21–23   Jesus' three great functions are: (1) Giver of life, (2) Bringer of judgment, and (3) Receiver of glory and honor.

25   "An hour is coming," is a figure of speech used in John's writings. It is usually juxtaposed with the statement "and is now." See verse 28 for the

(continued on next page)

is when the dead will hear the voice of the Son of God and the ones who hear will live. **26** For just as the Father has life in Himself, so to the Son He has given life in Himself. **27** And He gave Him authority to make judgment because He is the Son of Man.

28 "Do not be amazed at this for an hour is coming when all who are in the tomb will hear His voice **29** and come out. The ones who have done good things [will rise] to a resurrection of life. But the ones who have practiced evil [will rise] to a resurrection of judgment.

30 "From Myself, I do not have the power to do anything. As I hear, I judge, and My judgment is just because I do not seek My own will but the will of the One who sent Me.

31 "If I testify about Myself, My testimony is not true. **32** There is another one testifying about Me, and I know that his testimony about Me is true. **33** You have sent to John, and he has testified to the truth. **34** But I do not receive the testimony of man. I am saying these things to you that you might be saved.

35 "He was a lamp, burning and shining, and you chose to bask for a time in his light. **36** But I have testimony greater than John's. The work which the Father has given Me to finish, these works I do testify about Me, that the Father has sent Me. **37** And even the Father who sent Me has testified about Me.

"You have neither heard His voice nor seen His face. **38** You do not have His Word living in you because you do not believe the One He sent to you.

---

other half of this construction where Jesus says an hour is coming when the two resurrections will take place.

30 Jesus' judgment is God's judgment.

31 Here Jesus responds to the charge "What evidence can you give that your claim is true?" (See also Deut. 17:6; 19:15; 2 Cor. 13:1; and Matt. 18:16.) The four sources of testimony on Jesus' behalf are:

1. Self-testimony: He disclaims this testimony.
2. John's testimony: Valuable but insufficient because it is human testimony.
3. God's work: As seen in the healing of the crippled man. They cannot believe because such a sign still requires faith.
4. Scripture: They have degraded it by corrupting it with the oral tradition. "You do not have His Word living in you" (v. 38).

39 "You search the writings because you think life eternal is in them for you to have. [These writings] are the very ones who testify about Me. **40** Yet you do not want to come to Me so that you can have life.

41 "I do not receive glory from men. **42** But I know you, and you do not have God's love in yourselves.

43 "I have come in the name of My Father, and you do not receive Me. But if another comes in his own name, that one you will receive. **44** How are you able to believe? You receive glory from each other, but you do not seek the glory that comes from the only God.

45 "Do not think I will accuse you to the Father. There is [already] someone accusing you: Moses, the one all your hope is in. **46** If you really believed Moses, you would believe Me for he wrote about Me. **47** But if you do not believe what he wrote, how can you believe what I say?" ✄

The Pharisees once asked John the Baptist if he was "the Prophet," which John denied. "The Prophet like unto Moses" was a misunderstood figure in Jesus' day. No one seemed to understand that this prophet was a Messianic figure. The Pharisees' question indicates that the people seemed to think the Prophet was simply another precursor to the Messiah, like Elijah. However, throughout the Gospel of John, Jesus clearly identifies Himself as the fulfillment of this Old Testament prophecy.

---

39 This is not a command but rather a scathing comment.

45 The Pharisees called themselves the "disciples of Moses" and were extremely proud of their connection to him. Moses had entrusted the written law to the priests, and the Pharisees claimed that they were descendants of the "elders," to whom they said Moses had given the oral Law. To imagine themselves being accused before God by their own master Moses would have been unthinkable.

46 Jesus clearly makes the claim that the Pentateuch is a book that concerns itself with pictures of Christ as well as pre-Incarnate appearances of Jesus as the angel of the Lord. If the Pharisees are not able to grasp the central teaching of their rabbi, Moses, concerning the coming of Jesus, then no amount of testimony will convince them. A Word that had been directed specifically to them had been denied.

The hallmark of the Prophet was that he would speak only the words that God had placed in his mouth. Here, as in the rest of John's Gospel, Jesus insists that He only speaks what He has heard from the Father. This is the "work" the Father has given Jesus. Like the Prophet, Jesus is intent on telling them everything the Father has given Him to say.

The last important aspect of the Prophet is the warning God attaches to his person. Serious consequences will occur to those who do not listen to the Prophet. Jesus speaks of a time that is coming when two resurrections will take place. A resurrection of life and a resurrection of judgment. As is promised in the verse from Deuteronomy, the ones who have not listened to the Prophet will be guilty, simply for refusing to listen.

> The LORD said to me: "What they have spoken is good. I will raise up for them a Prophet like you from among their brethren, and will put My words in His mouth, and He shall speak to them all that I command Him. And it shall be that whoever will not hear My words, which He speaks in My name, I will require it of him." (Deut. 18:17–19)

Jesus mentions the writings of Moses, the Torah. The Pharisees, who called themselves "the disciples of Moses," prided themselves in their meticulous knowledge of Moses' writings. Jesus calls into question their motive for "searching" the writings. They think that life comes as a by-product of their laborious, searching efforts, their "works" related to the Scriptures. Jesus seems puzzled and frustrated that they refuse to come to Him to receive life.

The parting shot comes as Jesus reminds them that His role is not that of accuser; He will not accuse them before His Father. Lo and behold, their accuser will be the very one who is their hope, Moses! Their own great rabbi will expose their disbelief before the Father. This would have been unthinkable blasphemy for the Pharisees.

In essence, Jesus tells them, "He wrote about Me. If you do not believe what he wrote, how can you believe what I say?"

Like Moses, Jesus was perfectly faithful in speaking the Words of the Father to anyone who would listen, no matter what it might cost. It had been Moses' calling, and it was now the "work" of the Prophet as well.

JOHN 6

[HE] HAD RAINED DOWN MANNA ON
THEM TO EAT,
AND GIVEN THEM OF THE BREAD
OF HEAVEN.

PSALM 78:24

THE PEAH

JOHN
6:1–15

1 After these things, Jesus departed across the Sea of Galilee (that is Tiberias). **2** A great crowd was following Him because they saw the miraculous signs He was performing on the sick.

3 Jesus went up on a mountain and sat with His disciples. **4** Passover was near.

5 As He lifted up His eyes and saw the great crowd coming

Chapter 6 represents a turning point in the ministry of Jesus. The scandal of the gospel will be introduced most powerfully here.

2   John wants us to know that these are people who are curious about "miraculous signs."

4   This is the last Passover before the Cross. It is now one year to the Crucifixion.

5   Jesus asks Philip because he is from Bethsaida, which is only a couple of miles away. Some have speculated that Philip might have been the provider for the Twelve as Judas was the treasurer. *(continued on next page)*

toward Him He said to Philip, "Where can we buy bread so that these people can eat?" **6** (He was only saying this to test him for He knew what He was about to do.)

7 Philip answered Him, "Two hundred denari's worth of bread would not be enough for each one to take even a little bite."

8 Andrew, the brother of Simon Peter, one of the disciples, said to Him, **9** "There is a young boy here who has five barley loaves and two fish. But what are these among so many?"

10 "Make the people rest," Jesus said. There was a lot of grass in the place where the people rested. They numbered about five thousand.

11 Jesus took the loaves, and after He had given thanks He passed them out to the ones who were resting. He did the same with the fish. They all ate as much as they wanted.

12 When everyone was full, He told His disciples, "Gather the 'peah' so that nothing is lost."

The feeding of the five thousand is the only miracle of Jesus that appears in all four Gospels (see 2 Kings 4:42 where Elisha feeds one hundred).

6 One feature that separates John from the Synoptics is this backward-looking perspective. Only John takes us aside and whispers in our ear vital information he came to know only after the event he is describing.

Look for this unique feature to occur throughout the narrative. This information allows us to speculate as to the tone of his voice.

7 Philip's skepticism parallels that of Elisha's servant in 2 Kings. Andrew provides a contrast to them both. The situation seems hopeless.

ᴰ9 John gives us the detail that the bread was made of barley. This is meant to make the offering seem even more dismal, since the Mishna says that barley is food for beasts. When Roman soldiers were punished they were made to eat barley bread.

11 Note the subdued tone of the miracle. For Jesus, and for us, a miracle is nothing more and nothing less than answered prayer.

12 When Jesus says, "so that nothing is lost," He is invoking a rabbinic principle that unlocks the meaning of this miracle. "Great will be the punishment of those who waste the crumbs of food," the rabbis had said. The leftovers, the *peah,* was the portion left to the obedient slave that was traditionally collected after the banquet was over.

The word John uses for *basket* denotes not a large basket but a lunch-pail size. The significance of the miracle is not that there was a great abundance

(continued on next page)

13 So they gathered it up and filled twelve lunch baskets with the leftover pieces from the five barley loaves. **14** When the people saw the miraculous sign He did, they said, "This is truly the Prophet, the One who is to come into the world."

15 Jesus, knowing that they were about to come and force Him to become king, departed once again to the mountain alone. ✖

Jesus makes the four-mile trip by boat back across the lake with a crowd of curiosity-seekers in tow. Only one year of His earthly ministry is left, for the next to the last Passover is near.

John does not tell us if Jesus went to the mountain to spend some time alone with the Twelve. We know from other passages that He would call them away from the ministry from time to time to rest.

As He sees the herd of people approaching He asks Philip, who is a local, "Where might we get some food for the crowd?" Philip rightly sees the problem as not where can we get it but how in the world to pay for the food. It was only a test, however, but Philip failed to notice the ironical tone in Jesus' voice.

Andrew, like his brother Simon, often says more than he knows. The boy he has found seems to possess the only food for miles. The pressure is on. The people are starting to gather around.

"Make the people rest," Jesus says. "Let them sit down in the grass." Then, "Give Me the loaves and fish." Then He breaks the bread as He says, "Blessed art thou, Eternal God our Father, who causes bread to come forth from the earth." (This is the traditional rabbinic blessing at mealtime.)

---

of food left over (that is the point of the feeding of the four thousand [Mark 8:1–13]) but that there was exactly enough for each disciple to have a basket for himself. Each one was perfectly provided for.

14 The recognition by the people that Jesus was the Prophet like Moses comes from the fact that, like Moses, He had just given them bread in the wilderness. This is obliquely referred to again in verse 31.

15 Jesus knows the people only want to use Him. He refuses a moment's popularity, not wanting to be a "bread king" (see also v. 26).

Once again the miracle seems so ordinary, many scholars argue that no miracle took place at all. They say Jesus' example of generosity (though it was, after all, the little boy who was generous) so inspired the onlookers that everyone shared what little food he or she had with others. These interpreters say the miracle was one of generosity among the people and not a miraculous multiplication of the loaves.

This is the only miracle that all four Gospel writers saw as important enough to include in their narratives. If it had merely been an object lesson, as some believe, it is hard to imagine such significance being placed on the story.

Like the wine at Cana and the healing of the official's son, the miracle is subdued. It is only after all the people are full that they seem to realize a miracle has taken place at all. It was the miraculous sign they had been begging for, only not quite as miraculous as they had imagined.

"This man must be the Prophet, like Moses," the crowd concludes. Like Moses, He has given them bread in the wilderness. What could be clearer? Jesus has, for once, given the fickle crowd exactly what they wanted. If He is the Prophet, then we will make Him king, they thought. But as a dozen or so stronger, more zealous, members of the crowd begin to close in on the last-known location of Jesus, their minds bent on "convincing" Him to take up the scepter, they find that He has disappeared. No one, not even the disciples saw Him leave. They were all too busy, it seems, eating their fill.

One detail of the story is rarely discussed. Yet to me it is as important as the multiplication of the loaves.

In proper rabbinic form, Jesus instructs His disciples to gather up the leftovers, or *peah*. The fragments of bread that remained after the banquet were supposed to be saved and given to the servants. (No one gathered up the remains of the fish, and it is not hard to imagine why!) In those lean times wasting food was seen as ingratitude in the face of God's provision, as a sin. "Gather the *peah*," Jesus told them and another subtler miracle happened.

Philip had grabbed his purse, worried that eight months of his meager wages might have gone down the dark hole of the crowd's hunger. But after it was all over, he and the others found their lunch baskets full; the leftovers filled exactly twelve lunch-sized baskets. No more, no less.

To become a servant at the feast was all that was asked of them, and indeed is all that is asked of us.

A WALK ON
THE WATER

JOHN
6:16–24

16 As evening came His disciples went down to the sea **17** and put out in a boat. They were going across to Capernaum. It was dark. Jesus hadn't come back yet.

18 The sea was awakened as a mighty wind began to blow. **19** After they had rowed about three to three and a half miles they saw Jesus walking on the sea, coming near the boat. They were terrified.

20 But He said to them, "I AM; don't be afraid."

21 Then they were willing for Him to get into the boat. Immediately the boat landed at the place where they were going.

22 On the next day the crowd on the other side of the sea saw that only one boat was gone and that Jesus had not gotten into it, only His disciples. **23** Other boats came from Tiberias, nearby the place where they ate the bread after the Lord had given thanks. **24** When the crowd saw that Jesus and His disciples had gone, they set sail and came to Capernaum, looking for Jesus.

> Those who go down to the sea in ships,
> Who do business on great waters,
> They see the works of the LORD,

---

17   The incident of Jesus walking on the water is graphically prophesied in Psalm 107:23–30 (and also in Job 9:8–11 and 6:26).

20   Jesus literally calls out "I AM," the single name by which He can be recognized in the midst of this or any storm.

And His wonders in the deep.
For He commands and raises the stormy wind,
Which lifts up the waves of the sea.
They mount up to the heavens,
They go down again to the depths;
Their soul melts because of trouble.
They reel to and fro, and stagger like a drunken man,
And are at their wits' end.
Then they cry out to the LORD in their trouble,
And He brings them out of their distresses.
He calms the storm,
So that its waves are still.
Then they are glad because they are quiet;
So He guides them to their desired haven.

Psalm 107:23–30 ❧

To be in a boat at night in the middle of a storm is the best place to learn how small and power-less you really are. Jesus is not with His disciples, and it is dark, John tells us. The wind is whipping the waves into a storm.

John does not indicate that the storm is particularly frightening to the disciples, many of whom are seasoned fishermen. They keep pulling at their oars for a respectable three miles.

What frightened them, what really scared them, was not the storm but the sight of a figure walking toward them on the water, occasionally lit up by flashes of lightning. Where do you flee in the middle of such a storm when a ghost is heading straight for you?

We do not learn what they might have shouted above the roar of the wind. Perhaps they yelled at the apparition to simply go away.

Their fear and confusion vanished when they heard the sound of a familiar voice. "I AM; don't be afraid." John does not give the detail of the calming of the storm; rather he seems satisfied to have told us of the calming of the disciples instead.

Jesus asks us to look, not at the conditions that surround us, stormy as they may be. He only asks that we acknowledge His presence, the I AM of who He is. Even as He chose not to spare the disciples from their initial fear of the storm, so we are often left for a time to ride out the waves and listen for the sound of His voice.

THE SCANDALON

JOHN
6:25-71

25 After they found Him on the other side of the sea, they said, "Rabbi, when did You get here?"

26 Jesus answered them, "AMEN, AMEN, I say to you, you are looking for Me not because you saw miraculous signs but because you ate the loaves until you were full. **27** Do not work for food that spoils but for the food that lasts forever, which the Son of Man will give you. He is the One the Father has sealed to be sacrificed."

28 They said to Him, "What must we do so that we may work the works of God?"

29 "This is the work of God," Jesus answered. "Believe in the One He sent."

30 Then they said, "What sign will You perform then so

---

25   Characteristically Jesus does not answer the crowd's question.

27   Jesus alludes to Isaiah 55:2. The only word the people seem to hear is *work*.

The reference to the seal of approval sounds an ominous tone. Before a sacrifice could be offered it was inspected and marked with a seal. This meant that it was fit to be sacrificed.

M28   They have only heard the reference to work and typically miss the deep significance of what Jesus has just said. This is another example of the Motif of Misunderstanding.

29   Abraham is the example of the power of belief needed to achieve righteousness with God (see Gen. 15:6 and Rom. 4:3).

30–31   Jesus has just said that belief is the work God desires. They respond with a request to see Jesus do a work. They are only desirous of more bread. Like the woman at the well, Jesus will offer them bread that will end

(continued on next page)

that we may believe in You? **31** Our fathers ate manna in the wilderness, as it is written, 'He gave them bread from heaven to eat.'"

32 Jesus said, "AMEN, AMEN, I say to you, it wasn't Moses who gave you the true bread from heaven but My Father. Only He can give you the true bread from heaven. **33** For the Bread of God is the One who has come down from heaven to give Life to the world."

34 "Lord," they said, "from now on give this bread to us."

35 Jesus said to them, "I am the Bread of Life. Anyone who comes to Me never gets hungry, and whoever believes in Me will never get thirsty again. **36** But, as I told you, you have seen Me and you do not believe. **37** All that the Father gives to me will come, and whoever comes to Me I will never drive away. **38** I have come down from heaven, not to do My own will but the will of the One who sent me. **39** This is the will of the One who sent me: that I should lose none of those He has given Me but, on the last day, raise them up.

40 "This is the will of my Father; that all who see the Son

---

their hunger forever. The people are quoting a Targum, or ancient commentary, on Ecclesiastes when they refer to "what is written."

32   The Hebrew word for the bread the Israelites ate in the desert was *manna*. This is really not a word but rather a question mark followed by an exclamation point. The best translation is "What?!" The manna was, in fact, a picture of what was to come. It was not the real bread. These Jews still do not understand what the true bread is and might have also called Jesus "What?!" They wanted Him to provide a sign, to do a miracle. They didn't realize that He was the miracle; the Sign was standing there before them. He had come down from heaven. What more could be asked?

M34   Here's the Motif of Misunderstanding again. The people misunderstand, thinking Jesus is speaking of literal bread.

35   This is the first of the seven "I AM" sayings. Note that Jesus does not make this pronouncement until after He has validated His claim by feeding five thousand people.

36   Jesus had not come to give them bread. He had come to give them Himself.

38   This is an example of the Prophet like Moses motif.

39   Compare this with John 10:28: "None can pluck you out of My hand."

40   This is a simple, one-verse statement of the plan of salvation. John is famous for these.

and believe in Him may have life eternal. And, on the last day, I will raise them up."

41 The Jews began to murmur about Him because He said He was the bread that comes down from heaven. **42** They said, "Isn't this the man, Jesus, the son of Joseph, whose father and mother we know? How can He say He came down from heaven?"

43 "Stop murmuring among yourselves," Jesus answered. **44** "No one has the power to come to Me unless the Father who sent Me draws them. And, on the last day, I will raise them up."

45 "In the prophets it is written, 'They shall all become the ones taught by God.' Everyone who hears and learns from the Father comes to Me. **46** No one has seen the Father except the One from God, He has seen the Father."

47 "AMEN, AMEN, I say to you, the one who believes has life eternal. **48** I am the Bread of Life. **49** Your fathers ate manna in the wilderness and they died. **50** Here is the Bread which has come down from heaven that a person may eat and not die. **51** I am the Living Bread which has come down from heaven. If anyone eats this bread they will live into the age. And the bread which I will give for the life of the world is My flesh."

52 The Jews began arguing with each other, "How does He have the power to give us His flesh to eat?"

53 Jesus said, "AMEN, AMEN, I say to you, unless you eat the

---

41   The Greek word for "murmur" used here is the same one found in the Greek translation of the Old Testament *(Septuagint,* or LXX) for the children of Israel murmuring in the desert against Moses.

42   The scandal begins to build with this statement.

44   Dietrich Bonhoeffer said the call of God makes everything possible.

49   The principle of the manna is clear: Spiritual things are often revealed through the physical world.

51   Jesus as the Bread is "better than" because He is living. The same is true in that He provides the "living" Water. His sacrifice will be more acceptable because it is a living sacrifice.

52   The scandal builds.

53   These are not the words of someone who is trying merely to drum up followers. This is a repelling way to state a vital truth. So it is with us. We are first of all proclaimers of the truth and not salesmen trying to sell as many people as we can. Jesus is always the pattern for our action in the world.

(continued on next page)

flesh of the Son of Man and drink His blood you do not have life in you. **54** The person who feeds on My flesh and drinks My blood has Life Eternal. And, on the last day, I will raise them up.

55 "For My flesh is true food, and My blood is true drink. **56** The one who feeds on My flesh and drinks My blood stays in Me and I in him.

57 "As the Living Father sent Me and I live because of the Father, so the one who feeds on Me will live because of Me. **58** Who ever feeds on this Bread, which came down from heaven, will live into the age and not die like the fathers who ate the manna."

59 He said this while teaching in the synagogue in Capernaum.

60 Many of His disciples who heard this said, "This is a hard word. Who has the power to hear it?"

61 Jesus knew inwardly that His disciples were murmuring about this.

"Does this cause you to stumble?" He asked them. **62** "If you see the Son of Man going up into heaven where He was at first, what will you do then? **63** It is the Spirit that makes things alive. The flesh does not count for anything. The words I speak to you are Spirit and Life. **64** But some of you do not believe." (From the beginning Jesus knew who did not believe and who would betray Him.)

When you strip away the symbolic meaning these words have taken on over the past two thousand years and hear them as if for the first time, they are gruesome. Remember that Jesus is addressing a group of people who observe minutely intricate dietary laws.

57   Jesus does not soften the image but rather exaggerates it further. One of Jesus' great desires is that we might feed on Him. Why, then, do we often feel so starved? Because we are not regularly going to Him to be nourished by the only bread that truly satisfies.

59   The site of this synagogue has been extensively excavated.

60   These are not curiosity-seekers but rather disciples who can no longer bear the scandal. Their question expects the answer "No one can accept it."

63   This statement provides the framework through which Jesus' statements can be understood. That which is spiritual is the only thing that matters. The physical only counts insofar as it points to the spiritual.

ᴰ**64**   Note the unique backward-looking perspective of John.

65 He said, "This is why I told you that no one has the power to come to Me unless it has been given to them by the Father."

66 From then on many of His disciples went back [home] and no longer walked with Him.

67 Jesus said to the Twelve, "You do not want to go away, do you?"

68 "Lord," Simon Peter answered, "to whom would we go?
You have the Words of life eternal, 69 and we have believed and
know that You are the Holy One of God."

70 Jesus answered, "Didn't I choose you, the Twelve, and
one of you is a devil?" 71 (He was speaking of Judas of Simon
Iscariot, for he, one of the Twelve, was about to betray Him.) ⅋

He will be . . . a stone of stumbling and a rock of offense.
Isaiah 8:14

Just at the point when the people were following Jesus about in droves, when they desired to make Him king, He begins talking like a madman. His sayings had always been somewhat obscure, spiritual, metaphorical, but never anything like this.

The crowd found Jesus back in Capernaum. When they asked Jesus how He got there without the use of a boat He characteristically ignores their question and gets to the heart of the matter. They have come for bread, another free meal, and Jesus will have nothing to do with it.

---

65 In the face of such scandal the only ones who could possibly come to Jesus must be drawn by the Father through the scandal.

66 This moment represents an important turning point in the ministry. The scandal has begun to take effect.

67 This question expects a "no" answer. It could also be translated, "You don't want to leave, too, do you?"

68 In the tone of Peter's response to Jesus we hear the tension every believer is called to live in. The dilemma is that there is no place to go. The only true Lord is a scandal.

"Believe," He tells them. "That's all the work the Father requires of you." Like Abraham, believe.

But again they ask for a sign, which they hope will lead to another picnic in the grass. But that is not what following Jesus is.

All He has to offer them is Himself, the Bread that has come down from heaven. Yet, they have seen Him and still they do not believe. They keep asking for signs, failing to realize that He is the sign, the miracle, the One who has come down from heaven, the true Bread from heaven.

Even as the children of Israel murmured in the wilderness, so now the people begin to murmur when they hear Jesus talking about having come down from heaven. After all, they know His parents and even His grandparents. If He's from anywhere, it's Nazareth, and that isn't heaven!

"No one can come . . . unless the Father draws them," Jesus tells the grumbling crowd. God will teach them and they will come, and Jesus will raise them up on the last day.

This bread from heaven is alive, Jesus tells the crowd, and that is why it is better than the manna their fathers ate. It gives eternal life. The same was true of the "living water" Jesus promised the woman at the well. This bread and water satisfy for all eternity the deepest hunger and thirst of the soul. Jesus' sacrifice will be a better sacrifice because it is a living sacrifice. Our hope is a better hope because it is a living hope (see 1 Peter 1:23). We are, therefore, to offer our own bodies as "living" sacrifices (see Rom. 12:1).

The crowd is disappointed, disgruntled, confused, and most of all, hungry. They have been grumbling like tired, hungry children. Jesus' next words will instantly transform them into an angry mob.

The bread is alive, Jesus tells them. It is His own flesh.

Jesus' scandalous words reach our ears, having been filtered down through two thousand years of church history. But these first hearers belonged to a community that observed some of the most strict dietary laws the world has ever seen. They did not even eat pork! Now Jesus, this One they had hoped for as a king, was talking about cannibalism!

If ever an explanation was called for from Jesus it is now. A few words might have calmed them down and helped them understand His horrific statement. This was a time to choose His words with the utmost care.

And Jesus did. He selected words designed to have the most explosive effect. Not only are the people told that they must eat His flesh, He then goes on to say they must also drink His blood! To the few who might have been holding out hope for a metaphorical interpretation, Jesus says, "My flesh is true food, and My blood is true drink."

John does not record the response of the mob for us. Perhaps it was best left unsaid. Perhaps he felt it didn't need to be said because the outcome would have been clear and certain. Maybe he doesn't record a response because he wants to leave us to respond in our own way.

John does tell us about the reaction of Jesus' disciples. (It is interesting to realize that there were others besides the Twelve who were already recognized as disciples.)

"Hard words," they said.

"Does this cause you to stumble?" Jesus asked. He has been telling about the bread that has come down from heaven. Now He challenges the disciples, "If you see the Son of Man going up into heaven where He was at first, what will you do then?" And indeed some of them will be witnesses in little more than a year's time to His ascension.

When Jesus speaks of stumbling, He opens the door into a whole new world of understanding what it means to be one of His disciples. The word in Greek is *scandalizo;* it comes from the noun *scandalon,* which means "stumbling stone."

Isaiah had promised the Messiah would be such a stumbling stone. And a close look at the life of Jesus reveals that everyone who came close to Him stumbled.

It is easy to see how the Pharisees and Sadducees were offended by Jesus. Almost every time they appear in the Gospels they are calling Him names or complaining or laying traps for Him. Here in John 6 we see His own disciples offended, stumbling over the scandalous things He had said. In Mark 3 we read that early in His ministry Jesus' mother and brothers became convinced that He was out of His mind. They came, in fact, to take Him away.

Of all the people who were confronted by Jesus, John the Baptist should have been the last to stumble. John recognized the dignity of Jesus from his mother's womb. John first called Jesus, "the Lamb of God," and saw the Spirit descend like a dove. John heard the very voice of God declaring Jesus to be His Son. Yes, if anyone should have been immune to the offense it should have been John.

But even John is scandalized, for this is a part of coming close to Jesus. In Matthew 11 we read of John's disciples coming to Jesus with a remarkable question. John is in prison, wrongly arrested for speaking out against the adulterous relationship Herod was having with his brother's wife. From John's disciples we hear his question, "Are You the Messiah or should we look for someone else?"

John has stumbled. Jesus has failed to meet his expectations, not because there is anything wrong with Jesus but because John's expectation are wrong. It is hard not to sympathize with John. Who of us would expect to end our lives in prison, our heads chopped off and given to a dancing girl?

Jesus sends word back to His cousin, "Blessed is he who does not stumble because of Me" (Matt. 11:6).

Jesus would not have said this unless the prospect of stumbling over the scandal of Him was a reality.

There are only two possibilities after encountering Him, Jesus tells us. Either we stumble on the stone and are broken so that He might make us whole again. Or the *scandalon* comes crashing down on top of us, grinding us to powder (see Matt. 21:44). Either way, He is always the "stone that makes men stumble and a rock that makes them fall" (Isaiah 8:14).

As the other disciples walk away, Jesus turns to the Twelve. He asks if they intend to leave as well. It is Peter, always the first to speak, who responds dismally, "To whom shall we go?" There is no place else to go though; if there were Peter might be the first person to go there. That is the dilemma. There is no other person to go to but Him, in spite of the fact that He seems to be driving them away with His hard words.

He will fail to meet their expectations again and again in this last year of their ministry together. He will ultimately die on a cross, perhaps His greatest failure in their eyes, His greatest weakness. But

God will teach them that the pain, the failure, the disappointment, the stumbling are all a necessary part of the mystery. The leap of faith begins with a stumble.

"We believe, no, we *know* that You are the Holy One of God," Simon, himself a stone, says.

JOHN 7

WISDOM CRIES OUT LOUD
IN THE STREETS . . .
PROVERBS 1:20*

THE GOLDEN PITCHER

JOHN
7:1–44

1 After this Jesus walked about in Galilee. He did not want to walk through Judea because the Jews were seeking to kill Him. **2** The feast of Tabernacles was near.

In chapter 7 Jesus returns to Jerusalem for the feast of Tabernacles *(Sukkoth),* which is celebrated at the end of September. It is a festival of joy before God, who blesses crops (see Deut. 16:15) that was later Americanized into Thanksgiving.

The agricultural significance of the feast comes from the fact that during the harvest the workers lived in the fields in "booths," or in Hebrew *sukkoth.* The booths have a historical significance as well, for during the wilderness wanderings the people lived in similar "booths" (see Lev. 23:42).

The feast of Tabernacles is one of the big three festivals of Judaism, the other two being Pentecost *(Shabuoth)* and Passover *(Pesach).* In the ministry of Jesus we see two of the three great feasts fulfilled. Jesus goes to the cross on Passover. The Holy Spirit comes at Pentecost. Some believe the third feast will be fulfilled at the Second Coming since the return of Christ is graphically

(continued on next page)

3 His brothers said to Him, "Leave here and go to Judea so that Your disciples will also see the works You do. **4** No one who seeks publicity does anything in secret. If You are going to do these things, display Yourself to the world." **5** (They said these things because even His own brothers did not believe in Him.)

6 Jesus said to them, "The hour for Me has not yet arrived. Your time is always here. **7** The world does not have the power to hate you, but Me it hates because I give witness that its works are evil. **8** You go up to the feast. My time has not yet been fulfilled." **9** Having said this, He stayed in Galilee. **10** After His brothers went up to the feast He also went, not openly, but in secret.

11 The Jews who were looking for Him at the feast were saying, "Where is that man?"

12 There was a lot of murmuring about Him among the crowd. Some were saying, "He is a good man." Others said, "No, He deceives the crowd." **13** No one spoke openly about Him for fear of the Jews.

14 In the middle of the feast Jesus went up into the temple and began teaching. **15** The Jews were amazed and said, "How has this man come by His education? He never studied."

---

pictured throughout the Bible, especially in Revelation, as a harvest, and the feast of Tabernacles is known as the "feast of the ingathering."

1   We fail to realize that Jesus, like Paul, spent a good portion of His ministry under the threat of men who had taken religious oaths to kill Him.

3   In this verse Jesus' brothers taunt Him (see also Mark 3:21 where they are convinced that He is out of His mind). The last scandalous discourse of Jesus, which was about eating His flesh, indicated that He was not interested in simply being a public figure but in doing the Father's will.

4   Jesus' brothers say that no one who wants to be famous acts in secret. Perhaps this is one reason why Jesus goes "in secret" to Jerusalem in verse 10. By His actions He refutes what they said about Him.

11   John does a wonderful job of making us feel as if we are in the midst of the crowd. We become the ones who overhear all the various opinions about Jesus.

13   We will learn in chapter 9 that a formal ban *(cherem)* has been placed on Jesus. This means that anyone who is associated with Him will be banned from Jewish society.

15   The people are accustomed to rabbinic teaching, which is based on citation of other noted rabbis. A rabbi would demonstrate his having studied

(continued on next page)

16 Jesus said, "My teaching is not from Me but the One who sent Me. **17** If anyone wants to do His will he will recognize whether the teaching is of God or if I am speaking on My own. **18** The one who speaks on his own does so to seek glory for himself, but the One who seeks the glory of the One who sent Him, He is true, and nothing unrighteous is in Him.

19 "Hasn't Moses given you the Law? And none of you does what the Law says. Why are you seeking to kill Me?"

20 The crowd answered, "You have a demon. Who is seeking to kill You?"

21 Jesus answered them, "I did one work [on the Sabbath] and everyone was astonished. **22** Yet because Moses gave you circumcision (not Moses but the Fathers) you will circumcise a man on the Sabbath. **23** If a man can be circumcised on the Sabbath so that the Law of Moses will not be broken, why are you angry with Me because I made the whole person well on the Sabbath? **24** Do not judge according to the appearance of things, but make a correct judgment."

25 Some of the Jerusalemites said, "Isn't this the man they

---

by his ability to quote other rabbinic sources. Jesus' teaching lacks this feature. He does not quote other rabbis; He quotes the Father. This same observation will be made about the preaching of Peter and John (see Acts 4:13).

16   The Prophet like Moses (see Deut. 18). Like Moses, Jesus only speaks what the Father has taught Him. It is the defining characteristic of the Prophet. This motif is central to John's Gospel.

18   This statement might indicate that perhaps Jesus still bears in His heart the painful rebuke of His brothers.

19   These Jews were self-congratulatory about "having" the Law. Jesus points out the difference between having the Law and keeping the Law.

21   The word *astonished* in Jesus' statement does not imply that the people were surprised by the miracle He performed but rather that they were amazed that He would heal on the Sabbath, thereby breaking their oral law.

22   If it so happened that the eighth day after the birth of a Jewish boy fell on the Sabbath he was still circumcised on that day. Jesus pointed out that provision is made in the Law for certain work, namely work that leads to salvation.

25   This statement shows that there are two groups in the crowd. The first group is aware of the death threat. This group of Jerusalemites have inside information; they are "locals." This division will appear again at the

(continued on next page)

are seeking to kill? **26** Look, He speaks out in the open, and they are saying nothing to Him. Maybe the rulers truly know that this man is the Christ. **27** But we all know where this man is from. When the Christ comes, no one will know where He comes from."

28 While He was teaching in the temple area, Jesus shouted, "You know Me and you know where I'm from. I have not come on My own. But the One who sent Me is true. You do not know Him. **29** But I know Him because I am from Him and He sent me."

30 They were seeking to arrest Him. But no one laid a hand on Him because the hour for Him had not come yet. **31** Many from the crowd believed in Him. They said, "Whenever the Christ does come He will not do more miraculous signs than this man, will He?"

32 The Pharisees heard the crowd murmuring these things about Him, so the chief priests and Pharisees sent the temple guard to arrest Him.

33 Jesus said, "I am only with you a little time, then I am going away to the One who sent Me. **34** You will look for Me and not be able to find Me. Where I am you do not have the power to come."

---

end of the Gospel. Those who have come from outside Jerusalem will enter the city shouting "Hosanna!" The locals, who are known to the high priest and open to his coercion, will be the ones who shout, "Crucify!" (Often we hear of the fickleness of the crowd. This is probably not the case.) Two separate groups are in view.

27   The rabbis taught that three things were unexpected; stepping on a scorpion, stumbling on a godsend, and the coming of the Messiah. Their comment does not represent biblical teaching but rather popular rabbinic myths. The disciples, notably Peter, will demonstrate their exposure to some of these popular myths concerning the Messiah. Later the crowd will argue that the Messiah is not from Galilee but from Bethlehem. Some have embraced the myth and some the biblical prophecy.

28   Again, the Prophet like Moses speaks only what the Father has taught Him (see Deut. 18).

31   The Greek form of this question expects a "no" answer.

32   It is indeed unusual to see these two groups come together. Normally the priests, who were Sadducees, and the Pharisees were divided because of their differing theology. When confronted with Jesus, the Jews were forced to make a choice: accept His Messiahship (which they were not prepared to do) or charge Him with blasphemy. We are also left with only two choices.

35 The Jews said amongst themselves, "Where is this man about to journey that we will not be able to find Him? He will not go to those who are dispersed among the Greeks and teach the Greeks, will He? **36** What does this word He said mean, 'You will seek Me and will not find Me,' and 'Where I am you do not have the power to come'?"

37 Now on the last day, the "great day of the feast," Jesus stood and shouted, "If anyone is thirsty let him come to Me and drink. **38** Like the Scripture says, 'streams of living Water will flow out of the heart of the one who believes in Me.'"

39 (He said this about the Spirit which the ones who believed in Him were about to receive for as yet the Spirit had not been given since Jesus had not yet been glorified.)

40 Some of the crowd who heard these words said, "This man is truly the Prophet." **41** Others were saying, "This man is the Christ." But some said, "The Christ does not come from Galilee, does He? **42** Doesn't the Scripture say that from David's seed and

---

ᴹ**35** Once again there is blatant misunderstanding in the face of a spiritual pronouncement from Jesus. This represents the Motif of Misunderstanding.

37 On the last and greatest day of the feast of Tabernacles the high priest would meet a large congregation in front of the temple. Together they would make their way down to the pool of Siloam, chanting hallelujah psalms along the way (see Ps. 118:25: "O work Thou then salvation"). At the pool the priest would fill a large golden pitcher with water, then he would lead the crowd back to the front porch of the temple. There the pitcher would be poured out in front of the people to commemorate the provision of water in the wilderness. At that moment Isaiah 12:3 was quoted aloud: "Therefore with joy you will draw water from the wells of salvation." This is the context and the setting for Jesus' statement. Also, note the detail John provides that Jesus spoke in a "loud voice."

38 Jesus refers here to Isaiah 58:11.

ᴰ**39** Here John gives us a backward-looking perspective. Jesus is the source of the Spirit just as the rock was the source of the water. The key is that they both had to be struck.

40 The people see the likeness between Jesus, who promises to provide water, and Moses, who provided water in the wilderness.

41 The people were unaware that the Prophet and the Christ were the same person. The following verses reveal their further confusion.

42 Earlier (in v. 27) they were saying that when the Messiah came no one would know where He was from.

from the village of Bethlehem where David came from, the Christ will come?"

43 The crowd became divided because of Him. 44 Some wanted to arrest Him, but no one would lay their hands on Him. ✠

A *story from the past . . .*

It is said, "He who has not known the joy of Tabernacles, has never truly known joy." For this reason the feast of Tabernacles, or Sukkoth, is the favorite celebration of my wife, Suzanna, and me. In the courtyards, on corners, and even on the rooftops, you can see the ritual huts or lean-tos my people have constructed so that we might remember the wilderness wanderings of our fathers. At night we eat, huddled together in the cool fall air in our makeshift huts, look up into the starry face of the sky, and remember the memories of our ancestors.

In the wilderness the Holy One, blessed be He, gave us bread from heaven and water from the rock. The soles of our shoes never wore out. He guided us with His presence in the day and with fire in the night. What greater reason could there be for our people to rejoice? Our collective memories, after all, are our great strength against the despair of the present. They are our true source of joy.

The festival week had been a long one. Celebrations, banquets, seeing old friends again who had made the journey up to Jerusalem. Suzanna was tired but still held on to her excitement in anticipation for the last great day of Sukkoth.

We got to the temple as early as we could. The court was already beginning to fill with believers who desired to follow the high priest in the joyful procession.

"Where is he?" Suzanna said, her weariness finally giving way to impatience.

"He will come. He always has," was all I said.

Just then we heard the high, tinkling sound that told us the priest was approaching. From every tassel on his robe a tiny bell was ringing. It was, for us, the sound of approaching holiness. Suzanna and I strained to see him above the heads of the crowd.

He stood alone on the front porch of the temple. In his hand was the golden pitcher, which would be the focus of the morning's observance. The crowd burst into song as he held it aloft, smiling as he surveyed the impatient throng.

At once we all began to sing the great hallelujah psalms. "Oh work Thou then salvation," the whole crowd began to chant and wave palm branches. The high priest had vanished into the crowd, which began to file in behind him and walk down toward the pool of Siloam. Our excitement grew as we made our way down the street. "It is no wonder," I shouted to Suzanna, "that this day is called the day of the great hosanna!"

At last we were there, out of breath, standing beside Siloam, the pool at the end of the great tunnel Hezekiah had "sent" straight through the rock. Once again the high priest held high the golden pitcher and solemnly filled it to the brim with the clear, cool water from the pool.

Then back up the hill we went. Once I almost lost Suzanna in the crowd as she became so caught up in the celebration that she began to dance with the other women. We sang, we danced, and we wept with joy, both for what God had done and for what we all hoped He would do: Send us His Messiah.

We are a people, it seems, who live too much in the past or the future. We look back and celebrate the faithfulness of our God, and we look ahead to the coming of the Messiah. Perhaps He will invite us out of the past and the future to finally live with Him in the present.

Exhausted from the climb, dizzy with dancing, and out of breath from singing, we reached the temple court once again. Suzanna and I had made our way to the head of the joyful column, so we were now standing next to the high priest, close enough to touch him, if it had been allowed. With one voice the crowd shouted "Lift up thy hand!" and threw down their branches.

As the high priest lifted the golden pitcher so we could all see, it caught the sun and all but blinded us. He faced the west and poured out the water so we might remember that our God had given our fathers water from the rock. That was how we looked back.

Then the priest shouted, from the words of the prophet, "With joy you will draw water from the wells of salvation!" And you could feel the excitement spark through the crowd. These words perfectly connected the past with our future hope. This was how we looked ahead.

I was standing so close to the high priest that some of the water splashed on my feet. I remembered the striking of the rock in the wilderness and wondered if that water had wet the feet of my fathers as this water was now washing mine.

The next voice I heard came from behind me. It startled me out of my remembering and brought me into the present moment. It was loud, almost desperately loud in its tone. I could not see the face of the man who shouted, but I could make out His northern accent. He was somewhere in the middle of the crowd, but I could hear the words clearly.

"If anyone is thirsty," He cried, "let them come to Me now and drink. Whoever believes in Me, as the Scriptures have said, 'streams of living water will flow from the innermost part of their heart.'"

There was an awkward silence among the crowd and then a murmuring, which began to build in intensity. It seemed as if some of them knew who this man was.

"He is the Prophet."

"No, He is the Christ."

"He's not from Bethlehem. He's from Galilee."

"Galilee, hah!"

Most of the crowd, however, was shouting its outrage at hearing this blasphemy.

"The Nazarene," the high priest hissed through clinched teeth. "The guards were supposed to arrest Him. Where is the guard? This is just the sort of thing we were afraid might happen."

The Galilean was all we spoke about on the journey home, Suzanna and me.

"What do you think?" she asked, her face still fresh in its seriousness.

"Who can tell?" I answered as I opened the gate. "If the Prophet will truly be like Moses, wouldn't He give us water? But where is the rock that must be struck? And why don't the priests recognize Him? If He's sent from God wouldn't they know? And, after all, who knows the Scriptures better than the Pharisees?"

Suzanna took it all in, as she has a habit of doing, before she spoke again several moments later. She had just blown out the lamp and was getting into bed beside me when she said, "Yes, the priests should know and the Pharisees. But this Jesus seems to know something none of them do."

She was waiting for me to ask. "What, dear woman?" I said, half asleep.

"He seems to know how thirsty we truly are."

THE INCREDULOUS HULKS

JOHN
7:45–53

⁴⁵ Just then the officers of the temple guard, of the chief priests and Pharisees, came back. "Why did you not bring Him?" they asked.

⁴⁶ "No one has ever spoken like this," they answered.

⁴⁷ "You have not been deceived, too, have you?" the Pharisees answered. ⁴⁸ "None of the chief priests or Pharisees have believed in Him, have they? ⁴⁹ A curse on this mob which does not know the law."

⁵⁰ Nicodemus (the one who came earlier), one of their own number, said to them, ⁵¹ "Our law does not judge a man unless it hears him first and knows what he does, does it?"

⁵² They answered him, "Surely you're not from Galilee, too, are you? Look, you will see that a prophet does not come out of Galilee." ⁵³ Then they all went home. ✽

Earlier, in verse 32, the temple guard had been sent with special orders to arrest Jesus. The problem was not what He was saying as much as what the people had begun to say about Him: "Could He be the Messiah?"

---

52 Note that at the least provocation the Pharisees threaten Nicodemus. "Surely you're not from Galilee too, are you?" is a veiled accusation that Nicodemus had become a secret follower of Jesus. The very ones who were entrusted with the spiritual welfare of the people end up cursing the people.

This is one of the first times the Pharisees and Sadducees act together, and that is remarkable in itself because up until that moment they had nothing in common. Now they share a mutual hatred for Jesus.

We need to have a clear picture of just exactly who the temple guards were who were sent to arrest the "hick from Galilee." Not just anyone could be one of the temple guards. They were the elite, the finest, strongest, bravest warriors in Israel.

Just as the priests were only chosen from the tribe of Levi at one time (that was no longer the custom in Jesus' day) the temple guard came exclusively from the tribe of Benjamin because of Benjamin's legendary ferocity in battle. The war cry of Israel had always been, "After thee, O Benjamin" (Hos. 5:8). The Benjaminites were always the first to charge into any fight. The temple guard was handpicked from this warrior tribe. Size, physical prowess, and zeal were the characteristics of the men sent to arrest Jesus.

By the time they return, after the scene in the temple court is over, it is easy to forget they had been sent (in v. 32), but now they have returned empty-handed, in violation of a direct order from the high priest himself.

"Well, why didn't you bring Him in?" the priest asks. The response comes from the lips of men who have grown up around the temple and have heard the priests speak since they were small boys. "No one has ever spoken the way He speaks," they stammer.

Perhaps they had formed a circle around Him in the crowd and were ready to strike in military fashion when Jesus shouted out. What is clear is that any one of them could have overpowered Jesus physically, much less a detachment of them. Instead they found themselves overpowered by His words!

The priests respond with accusations. They can't believe their own guard has been duped. "None of us have believed in Him!" they accuse, not knowing that Nicodemus, who is about to speak up, has most likely already given in to Jesus' call. And when Nicodemus does speak up, they turn on him, too, accusing him of becoming a "Galilean" as well. "Look into it," they challenge Nicodemus, "and you will find that a prophet does not come out of Galilee."

Their rage must have confused their memories. To a man, they would have known that indeed there was a prophet from Galilee—Jonah, the unwilling servant of God who spent three days in the belly of the great fish, just as this other Prophet from Galilee would spend three days in the belly of the earth.

The priests and Pharisees missed their chance to arrest Jesus without a struggle. From now on it will become increasingly difficult as the crowds around Him grow larger. In time, taking Him might result in a riot.

The Pharisees and priests leave, stamping their feet in anger. Nicodemus wanders out into the night, where we first met him. The guards walk out, too, still dazed by it all, their meaty hands scratching underneath their helmets as they wonder what might become of them now. Yet they were still willing to follow orders, to go to their deaths to defend the holiness of the temple, to send to their deaths any Gentiles caught going past the low wall that separated their area of the temple court from the Jews, to follow every order the high priest might give—except one.

STONES IN THE MORNING LIGHT

JOHN
8:1–11

¹ Jesus went to the Mount of Olives. ² At dawn He came back to the temple, and all the people came to Him. ³ Just as He sat down to teach, the scribes and Pharisees led in a woman who had been caught committing adultery. They made her stand in the middle of everyone.

The story of the adulterous woman appears in different places in various texts of John's Gospel. Most often, and in the oldest texts, it cannot be found at all. In one ancient source it even appears in the Gospel of Luke. The story was extracted, it seems, early in the transmission of the text. Its proper place is now for the most part lost. The copiers or their communities were afraid

(continued on next page)

4 "Teacher," they said to Him, "this woman has been caught in the very act of committing adultery. **5** In the Law, Moses commanded to stone this kind of woman. What do You say?"

6 (They were saying this to trap Him, so that they could have something to accuse Him of.)

But Jesus knelt and wrote down something on the ground. **7** As they continued questioning Him, He straightened up and said to them, "The one among you who is without sin, let him throw the first stone at her."

---

that it seemed Jesus was being "soft" on adultery, which was a particular problem in the early church. Jesus did condemn adultery but not the woman who discovered His grace. "He would not condemn her because he would be condemned for her," Frederick Buechner said.

In the brief span of eleven verses we have a crystalline picture of the forgiving love of Jesus. When we come to the end of the story, we feel as if we have read an entire book about the love of God.

5 Notice the continual emphasis on Moses. The basis for the Pharisees' charge is Leviticus 20:10 and Deuteronomy 22. They are in error about the stoning. The Torah merely says that the adulterer "shall be put to death."

6a This verse illustrates again John's backward-looking perspective. The Pharisees think they have laid a trap for Jesus. If He answers either a yes or a no, He is in trouble with either the Jews or the Romans. If He says no then He will be perceived as a lawbreaker. If He says yes then He will be in trouble with Rome since the empire had taken away from the Jews the power to pass a death penalty.

This backward perspective, so prevalent in the writings of John, is another indication that this passage was written by the evangelist and belongs in the Gospel.

ᴰ6b Jesus' writing on the ground is a fascinating eyewitness detail, another hallmark of John's writing style. The Greek word *katagraphein* literally means to "write down" and connotes a process of listing. One ancient variant text tries to express this idea by saying, "He was writing with his finger on the earth to declare their sins and they were seeing their secret sins on the stones." To gain further perspective on Jesus' actions, consider Jeremiah 17:13: "All who forsake You will be ashamed. All who turn away will have their names written in the dust, for they have forsaken the Spring of living Waters."* In the previous chapter Jesus described Himself as the living Water. Also note that He has just stated that He has come to reveal the world's sin.

7 In the face of this seeming dilemma, Jesus relies on a Wisdom text, Proverbs 20:9: "Who can say, 'I have made my heart clean, I am pure from my sin'?" Perhaps this reliance on the Wisdom literature is a further indication that John was the writer of this story.

⁸ Again, He knelt and wrote down something on the ground. ⁹ Those who heard left one at a time, beginning with the older ones first, leaving Jesus alone with the woman.

¹⁰ Jesus straightened up and said to her, "My dear, where is everyone? No one condemned you?"

¹¹ She said, "No one, Lord."

"Neither will I condemn you," Jesus said. "Go, and from now on stop sinning." 🞟

A *story from the past . . .*
I thought she was one of the most beautiful women I had ever seen. Little did I know the part she would have in changing my life.

I knew she was married. I also knew that the marriage was not working. This, of course, made her all the more attractive to the kind of man I was then. I started greeting her in the marketplace. At first she ignored me, as well she should; but after a time she acknowledged my presence. And after still more time we became friends.

She said her husband was threatening to hand her the *gittim,* the divorce papers. She would be outcast. Her only reason for any happiness was that they had no children, which was why he was divorcing her in the first place.

My marriage was also in the midst of a barren place. It had been years since my wife and I had been even remotely happy. The last evening, before the great shaking up of my life, my wife had asked me to leave the house altogether.

As I wandered the streets, wondering where I would sleep that night, I heard her. She had also been thrown out and sat next to a small pool, weeping.

She looked up through her tears, recognizing my face. I spoke kindly, seeking to comfort her, seeking to comfort myself. Before I knew it we were embracing one another, still weeping.

---

11 When Jesus says He will not condemn the woman He is validating what He will soon say: "I did not come to judge the world but to save it." In the Gospel of John, Jesus will always validate His words by His actions.

"I know a place," I whispered, and she understood.

They broke down the door just as it was getting light outside. We were still in bed together, just as they hoped they might find us. We were embarrassed, ashamed at what we had done, miserable, the both of us. They exuded a strange kind of satisfaction that bordered on happiness. We were a prize they had captured.

"You're coming with us!" they shouted at her. "Cover yourself."

As I rose to follow, one of them pushed me back onto the bed. "Disappear," he hissed.

They rushed her out the door and down the alley toward the temple. I will never forget the look on her face as they forced her outside. She was looking for help. I was looking only to hide.

I sat for a while, wondering what to do. Would my wife find out? What would my children think? I decided to follow at a safe distance in case my name came up in the trial.

I arrived at the temple just as a crowd had gathered around her. They were talking to someone I could not see from my place at the back of the crowd. He was sitting on the ground. I thought He must be a scribe, and they were asking about the proper procedure. I was thankful for once that the Romans had taken control of us; otherwise she would be lying dead by now under a heap of stones.

They had stopped by her house on the way to the temple to inform her husband. I later found out he was not willing to come and face his own humiliation. I heard he turned away from her, ignoring her pleas for help and forgiveness.

As I pushed through the crowd, taking care not to get so close as to be recognized, I could just make out their words.

The men who were standing kept asking the same question of the man seated on the ground. "Should we stone her?" they kept repeating.

Finally He stood up so that I could see His face clearly. He looked bemused. Their insistence was irritating Him, yet still He smiled faintly, as if He knew their true motives.

"Yes, by all means," he said. "Let's stone her."

She gasped. They seemed satisfied. I was sick.

"Let the first stone be thrown by the man who is without sin," He shouted as He picked up a dangerously big rock. He held it out to the ones who had dragged in the woman. Then He looked straight at me, extending the stone.

I looked away, disgusted with myself. When I looked back, I could no longer see Him. He was sitting on the ground where He had been at first. He was writing with His finger in the dust. Forgetting the risk, I moved to the front of the crowd for a better look.

There in the dust, at the top of a long list of names of the men who stood around, I read my own name and beside it the word "adulterer." *He knew!* And now they all knew.

There followed the dull thud of a dozen or more stones hitting the ground. We turned in silence and walked away, the older men leaving first.

I stopped and looked back at the two of them as I reached the gate. She was standing alone, shivering, in front of the man, who was just getting to His feet.

"Where did everyone go?" He asked, smiling. "Didn't anyone condemn you?"

"No," she whispered, looking down. "No one, Sir."

He took her chin in one of His hands. "I don't condemn you either," He said with a tender smile.

Then He became serious. He spoke as a parent disciplining a child. "Now go, and stop sinning."

She began to weep, not from shame as before, but from relief. He had saved her life. He had returned to her what the others, especially I, had stolen. She was sorry, painfully sorry. At last she had found Someone who could bear her sorrow for her.

I went straight home and confessed everything. My wife took upon herself the burden of forgiving me as best she could. We agreed to start over.

I heard the woman and her husband never reconciled. She asked for forgiveness and promised to make good her vows, but her husband could not find it in himself to make complete restoration.

The last time I saw her I was with my family at a gathering of His followers. They called us "Nazarenes" in those days. I almost didn't recognize her. She was standing with a group of women who traveled with Jesus and the Twelve to take care of them. I tried to get her attention, but her gaze was focused on the One who had saved her.

It was my wife who first came to believe in Him. She had heard Him speak about loving your enemies and forgiving the ones who use you. It was Jesus who gave her the strength to forgive me, the one who had used her. In the Nazarene she found not only forgiveness for her own sins but the power to finally forgive me.

LIGHT OF THE WORLD

JOHN
8:12–59

¹²Jesus spoke to them again saying, "I am the Light of the World. The one who follows Me will never walk in the darkness but will have the Light of Life."

¹³The Pharisees said, "If You testify about Yourself, Your testimony is not true."

¹⁴Jesus answered them, "If I testify about Myself My testimony is true, because I know where I came from and where I am

---

12   In this verse Jesus continues the discourse on His deity. The "I AM" statement prepares us for the healing of the man born blind in chapter 9. Again, in John's Gospel, Jesus will always validate what He says about Himself by His actions.

Light was another name for the Messiah (see Isa. 9:1–2; 42:6; and 49:6; and Mal. 4:2). If the story of the woman has been misplaced here, then it is still the first day of the feast of Tabernacles (7:37). If this is so, then Jesus' words may be connected to a celebration that took place on this day. During this "celebration of joy for the Law" the books of the Law were taken out of the ark in the temple and replaced by a single candle in allusion to Proverbs 6:23 and Psalm 119:105 (see also Isa. 9:2 and 60:1). In a rabbinic commentary on Numbers *(Bamidbar Rabba)* the prayer was prescribed for this occasion: "O Lord of the universe, Thou commandest us to light the lamps to Thee, yet Thou art the Light of the World." This might be another graphic example of Jesus' pointing to older tradition as foreshadowing.

During the rest of the chapter Jesus seems preoccupied with giving significant promises to His followers, and here we encounter the first one. Whoever walks with Jesus will never be in the dark but will have the Light of Life.

13   A discussion similar to this one has already taken place in John 5:31 concerning evidence. The Pharisees have in mind Deuteronomy 17:6; 19:15; and Numbers 35:30.

14   Jesus responds by implying that His word is authoritative.

109

going. But you, you do not know where I came from or where I am going. **15** You judge according to the flesh. I do not judge anyone. **16** But even if I do judge, My judgment is true because I am not alone. **17** In your law it is written that the testimony of two men is true. **18** I am one who testifies about Myself and the other is the Father who sent Me."

19 They said to Him, "Where is Your Father?"

"You do not know Me or My Father," Jesus answered. "If you had known Me, you would have also known My Father."

20 (These words He spoke in the treasury while He was teaching in the temple. But no one arrested Him because the hour had not yet come for Him.)

21 Therefore Jesus said again, "I am going away and you will look for Me and die in your sin. Where I am going you do not have the power to come."

22 The Jews said, "Surely He won't kill Himself, will He? After all, He did say 'Where I am going you do not have the power to come.'"

---

15   Jesus has just graphically demonstrated what He urges in this verse by how He deals with the woman.

18   Again note "the Father who sent Me." Jesus is the "sent" One.

ᴹ**19**   This could be an example of the Motif of Misunderstanding. Jesus has been speaking of the spiritual reality of God the Father. The people grossly misunderstand and ask to see Jesus' earthly father.

ᴰ**20**   The detail of the place of the incident must be significant. Perhaps it is meant to refer to the place where a large golden candelabra stood in the court of the women. It was lighted during the feast of Tabernacles in an observance called "the Illumination of the Temple."

The only reason John gives for Jesus' escape from the angry crowd is that "His time had not come yet." Every time we hear this statement we should understand that it implies a time is coming for Jesus.

21   Jesus' words are a reference to the prophetic mandate in Ezekiel 3:18 where the prophet was given the responsibility to tell the people about their sin. If he was obedient in this, he would not be guilty of their sin and they in turn would "die in their sin." Jesus has said He has come to convict the world of sin. The bizarre twist on this Old Testament concept is that in the end Jesus will indeed choose to suffer the penalty for the sins of the world.

ᴹ**22**   Here's the Motif of Misunderstanding again. The people misunderstand Jesus' passion and frustration. They seem to think this One who is promising the Light of Life has become suicidal.

23 He went on to say, "You are a part of the things which are below; I am of the things above. You are of this world; I am not of this world.

24 "I told you that you will die in your sins if you do not believe that I am. You will die in your sins."

25 They said to Him, "Who are You?"

"Why should I speak to you at all?" Jesus said. **26** "I have much to say and judge concerning you. But the One who sent Me is true. What I hear from Him, these things I speak to the world." **27** (They did not know that He was speaking to them about the Father.)

28 "When you 'lift up' the Son of Man," Jesus said, "then you will know that I am, and that by Myself I can do nothing. The things I say to you are just as the Father taught Me. **29** The One who sent Me is with Me. He has not left Me alone because the things I do always please Him." **30** (As He was saying these things many believed in Him.)

31 To the Jews who believed in Him Jesus said, "If you remain in My word, you are truly My disciples. **32** And you will know the truth. And the truth will free you."

33 But they answered Him saying, "We are of the seed of Abraham and have never been enslaved to anyone. What do You mean when You say we will become free men and women?"

---

24 Jesus is not speaking as a condemning judge but as the Light. He is seeking not to judge but to illuminate.

26b This verse illustrates the Prophet like Moses motif (see Deut. 18).

ᴰ**27** With his typical backward perspective, John informs us of the true mind-set of the crowd.

28 Note that the metaphor "lifted up" always refers to crucifixion and not to praise.

30 Despite the confusion, many still find faith in Christ.

31 Note that this second major promise is directed specifically to "the Jews who believed in Him." This is a promise for believers. The truth of which He speaks is not some general understanding of what is true, but rather the truth that Jesus is the Son of God. Jesus did not come to give us truths but Himself.

33 Jesus' vague implication concerning their freedom seems to set the Jews off. Josephus said, "They have an inviolable attachment to liberty." To even suggest to a Jew that he was a slave was a deadly insult.

34 "AMEN, AMEN, I say to you," Jesus said. "Everyone who sins is a slave to sin. **35** The slave does not remain in the house into the age. **36** The Son, however, remains into the age. So, if the Son frees you, you will really be free. **37** I know you are of Abraham's seed, but you seek to kill Me because My word has no place in you. **38** I am speaking of the things I have seen with the Father. You do the things you hear from your father."

39 They answered, "But our father is Abraham!"

"If you were Abraham's little children," Jesus said to them, "you would have been doing the works of Abraham. **40** But, in fact, you are seeking to kill Me, a man who has simply told you the truth, which I heard from God. Abraham did not do this. **41** You are doing the work of your father."

"We have not been born out of fornication. We have one Father, God!"

42 Jesus said, "If God were your Father, you would have loved Me. I came from God, and here I am. I have not come for Myself but for the One who sent Me. **43** And so why is it that you do not recognize My speaking? It is because you are not able to hear My word. **44** You are of your father, the devil, and you want to do the desires of your father. He was a murderer from the beginning. He cannot stand the truth because the truth is nowhere in him. When he lies he speaks of his own things because he is a liar and the father of it.

---

34 Here Jesus radically redefines slavery and freedom.

36 This is the third major promise.

40 When Jesus appeared to Abraham as the Angel of the Lord in Genesis 18, He was welcomed.

41a Jesus has pulled the rug out from under them with this statement. First He took away their freedom status and called them slaves. Now He has annulled their descent from Abraham.

41b This might be a slap in Jesus' face. There were later rumors spread about Him that He was the illegitimate son of a Roman soldier.

44a In *Sohar Kadesh,* a rabbinic document from Jesus' time, the wicked are called "the children of the old serpent who slew Adam and his descendants."

44b The two essential qualities of the devil that must be understood are: (1) He is a murderer, and (2) He is a liar.

45 "But because I speak the truth, you do not believe. **46** Can anyone among you expose any sin in Me? Then if I speak the truth, why do you not believe Me? **47** Whoever is from God hears the words of God. You do not hear because you are not from God."

48 The Jews answered Him saying, "Are we not right in saying that You are a heretic and that You have a demon?"

49 "I do not have a demon," Jesus answered. "I honor My Father. You dishonor Me. **50** I am not seeking glory for Myself. There is One seeking and judging.

51 "AMEN, AMEN, I say to you, if anyone keeps My word, he will not see death into the age."

52 "Now we know You have a demon," the Jews said. "Abraham died, didn't he, and the prophets? Yet You say if anyone keeps Your word they will never taste death into the age. **53** You are not greater than our father, Abraham, are You? He died. The prophets died. Just who are You making Yourself out to be?"

54 Jesus said, "If I glorify Myself, My glory is nothing. It is My Father, whom you say is your God, who glorifies Me. **55** You have not known Him. But I have known Him. If I were to say I have not known Him, I would become like you, liars. But I do know Him, and I keep His word. **56** Your father Abraham was glad that he could see My day. He saw it and rejoiced."

57 "You are not even fifty years old," the Jews said, "and You have seen Abraham?"

58 "AMEN, AMEN, I say to you," Jesus said, "before Abraham ever was, I AM."

---

46   This might be a reference back to the incident with the woman accused of adultery.

48   *Samaritan* and *heretic* were synonymous. This might also be a garbled form of the name Shameron, the prince of demons. They have attributed Jesus' work to Satan (see Mark 3).

51   The final stunning promise. In 11:25 Jesus will try to explain this to Martha.

58   Jesus has spoken the unspeakable Name. When Moses asked God His name in Exodus 3:14 He told Moses to say "I AM has sent me to you."

59 They picked up stones to throw at Him. But Jesus hid and left the temple. ✵

Whenever John gives us a specific detail there is good reason. The setting of this story, he tells us, is the temple treasury. This was a place where it seems Jesus liked to linger, perhaps because it was the most public area of the temple complex. In Luke 21 Jesus watches the widow drop her last two cents into one of the trumpet-shaped offering boxes.

There were four golden menorah in this area, which were lighted on the first day of the feast of Tabernacles. Jesus chooses this particular time and place to first make the pronouncement that He is the "Light of the World." Placed alongside Jesus' words of the previous chapter, saying He was the source for the living Water, we begin to get a feeling for the connectedness of Jesus' revelation to the Jewish rituals. These observances were truly meant to prepare the people to meet the Messiah.

"Light" was one of the names for the Messiah (see Isa. 9:1–2; 42:6; and 49:6; and Mal. 4:2). On the last day of Tabernacles the scrolls were removed from the ark in the temple and a single candle was placed inside in reference to two Wisdom passages, Proverbs 6:23 and Psalm 119:105. The prescribed prayer for this occasion was, "O Lord of the universe, Thou commandest us to light the lamps to Thee, yet Thou art the Light of the World." These words were still echoing in the temple as Jesus made His pronouncement. He will validate His claim in the next chapter by healing a man who was born blind.

Contained in the following verses describing yet another legal discussion as to the legitimacy of testimony and the right of passing judgment are some of the most significant promises Jesus has given. It is important that they come precisely at a time when some of the Jews are beginning to believe in Him. There are four:

1. Verse 12: "The one who follows Me will never walk in the darkness but will have the Light of Life."

2. Verse 31: "If you remain in My word, you are truly My disciples. And you will know the truth. And the truth will free you."

3. Verse 36: "If the Son frees you, you will really be free."

4. Verse 51: "If anyone keeps My word, he will not see death into the age."

Jesus promises these freedoms: freedom from the darkness, freedom from all that is untrue, and freedom from death itself. He promises the kind of freedom that only the Son is able to grant.

Being Abraham's descendants is not enough, Jesus tells them. Besides, their resemblance to Abraham is shaky at best. Abraham's children would have welcomed Jesus just as their "father" had welcomed the mysterious "Angel of the Lord" (see Gen. 18). "Abraham," Jesus says, "rejoiced at the mere thought of seeing My day." In contrast, these people are trying to kill Him, the man who is only attempting to tell them the truth that will set them free. Their actions cause them to bear a more striking resemblance to the devil.

The crowd hurls back the accusation that it is Jesus who is possessed by a demon. (A similar occurrence recorded in Mark's Gospel led to the pronouncement concerning the "unpardonable sin," which also involved the crowd accusing Jesus of being in league with the devil.) Earlier Jesus took away their freedom when He told them they were slaves to sin. Next, He annulled their descent from Abraham. Now, He has made a connection between their "works" and the devil. All this is becoming intolerable to the Jews.

Jesus has offered them life. The devil, He tells the crowd, is a murderer. The devil is the liar, He says, and the father of lies. The choice is clear. It has been illuminated for them by the Light of the World. They are free to come to the Light—or remain in the darkness.

In response to their question, "Just who do You think You are?" Jesus tells them He is the One whose prophesied coming caused Abraham to rejoice. They misunderstand. How could such things be possible? How could a thirty-year-old man have seen Abraham?

"Before Abraham ever was," Jesus said, "I AM."

When Moses had asked God to tell him His name in Exodus 3:14 so that the elders of Israel might recognize his words as authentic, the enigmatic response was, "Tell them I AM sent you." Amidst the many titles God gives us in the Old Testament to call Him by, there is really only one name: I AM. When Jesus spoke the Name,

115

they should have responded in worship. Instead, they did not recognize Him, as John told us in the prologue. Only when He was "lifted up," Jesus said, would they realize He was the One He claimed to be.

As the chapter began with the threat of a stoning, so it closes with the people picking up rocks to stone Jesus. This context of a threat to His life will follow Jesus throughout the remainder of the ministry.

The Motif of Misunderstanding sets Him apart, alone. He is the Light; the people choose darkness. He speaks the truth that sets them free; they choose the lie. He offers life; they fall in behind the murderer. He promises living Water; they prefer to dig their own cisterns. He will give His flesh as bread for them to eat; they will take His flesh and nail it to a cross.

ILLEGAL SABBATH SPIT

JOHN
9:1–41

¹ As he passed by, Jesus saw a man who was blind from birth. ² His disciples asked Him, "Rabbi, who sinned, this man or his parents, that he was born blind?"

This is the only instance of Jesus healing someone stricken from birth. This healing comes after Jesus' claim to be the Light of the World.

1   "As he passed by," is a loose chronological connector for John.

2   The rabbis taught that it was possible for someone to commit a sin while still in the womb and so suffer for it at birth. In the rabbinic material there is mention of a baby being born with a deformity because its mother walked through a pagan grove of trees and "delighted." So the disciples are asking if this man's deformity is due to some prenatal sin of his own or that of his parents.

As naive as this might sound, we tend to think in similar ways. John wants us to understand that the meaning of suffering is much deeper than a determination of cause and effect.

3 Jesus answered, "Neither has this man sinned nor his parents. This happened so that the works of God might be displayed in him. **4** While it is day, I must do the work of the One who sent Me. Night is coming when no one can work. **5** As long as I am in the world, I am the Light of the World."

6 Having said this, He spat on the ground and made clay out of the saliva and put the clay on the blind man's eyes.

7 He said to him, "Go, wash in the pool of Siloam" (which is translated *Sent*). He went and washed and could see.

8 The neighbors and those who saw him before as a beggar said, "This is not the one who sat begging."

9 Some said, "It is him."

Others said, "No, he only looks like him."

---

3 Jesus sees suffering as an opportunity for the power of God to be displayed in our lives. In Exodus 14:17, God states that He will get glory from the suffering caused by Pharaoh. John would have us learn to examine our own hurts in this light.

6 Jesus' action of making the mud and placing it on the man's eyes has received a number of different interpretations. Most run something like this: Jesus puts mud on his eyes to raise his expectations by doing something he would expect a "healer" to do. By so doing, Jesus helps the man's faith. Some say His actions are completely symbolic—Jesus, the Creator who first makes man from the dust, now uses dirt to recreate a man's eyes. Jesus applies saliva to a man's eyes in Mark 8, but it is not mixed with dirt. Also this healing was purposely done "out of town" and not in public. The previous explanations might serve better in the case of Mark's account.

The explanation here is much simpler. The answer is seen in the Pharisees' preoccupation with the fact that Jesus makes mud, thus violating the oral law. Within the scrupulous theology of the rabbis this could be construed as work, and, in their minds, a violation of the first commandment. Jesus spits and makes mud to purposefully break the oral law—which the Pharisees had added on to the biblical commandments—in the same way He commanded the lame man to carry his mat on the Sabbath.

7 Jesus sends the man to the pool of Siloam (which John dutifully translates for his Gentile readers to mean *Sent*). The pool was so called because it was the result of an underground tunnel, which was cut, or "sent," through solid rock. This is the same tunnel Hezekiah dug in 2 Chronicles 32; Isaiah 22; and 2 Kings 20.

9 The exchange between the healed man and his old friends seems almost comical.

But he said, "It *is* I!"

10 So they said to him, "How were your eyes opened?"

11 The man answered, "The man called 'Jesus' made clay and put it on my eyes and said to me, 'Go to Siloam and wash.' I went and washed and I saw."

12 They said to him, "Where is He?"

He said, "I don't know."

13 They led the once-blind man to the Pharisees. **14** (The day on which Jesus made the clay and opened his eyes was a Sabbath.) **15** So the Pharisees also asked him once more how he saw.

He told them, "He put clay on my eyes and I washed and now I see."

16 Because of this, some of the Pharisees said, "This man is not from God for He does not keep the Sabbath."

Others said, "How could a man who is a sinner have the power to do such signs?"

So there was a division among them.

17 Again they said to the blind man, "It was your eyes He opened. What do you say about Him?"

He said, "He is a prophet."

18 The Jews did not believe that he had really been blind until they called the parents of the one who could now see. **19** They

---

14 Note John's reference to Jesus making the mud before the mention of the healing. A gasp from the Jews should be heard when John states that this all took place on the Sabbath.

15ff. The dialogue is based on the same problem of evidence. The Pharisees will not accept this new evidence, so they will not accept Jesus' testimony (8:12ff.), John's testimony, God's work, or the Scriptures (5:31).

16 It is crucial to see the Pharisees' first response focuses on Jesus making the mud, as if there were no miracle at all. He made mud on the Sabbath; therefore He couldn't be from God. In John 7:21 Jesus says that He did one miracle and they were all astonished. What He means is that they were astonished, not by the miracle, but by the fact that He had done work on the Sabbath.

Here again John points out that the crowd was divided because of Jesus (see 7:43).

18–23 The man's parents are called in to testify. First their testimony is called into question: "This is your son, who is the one you say was born

(continued on next page)

asked them, "This is your son, who you say was born blind. How is it that he can see now?"

20 So his parents answered, "We know that this man is our son, and we know that he was born blind. **21** But how it is that he can see, we do not know. Neither do we know who it was who opened his eyes. Ask him. He is of age and so can speak for himself." **22** (His parents said these things because they were afraid of the Jews for they had already agreed that anyone who confessed Him to be the Christ would be banned from the synagogue. **23** This is why his parents said, "He is of age, ask him.")

24 A second time they called the man who was blind and said to him, "Give glory to God! We know that this man is a sinner."

25 The man answered, "If He is a sinner, I do not know. I only know one thing. I was blind; now I see."

26 So they said to him, "What did He do to you? How did He open your eyes?"

27 He answered, "I already told you, and you didn't listen. Why do you want to hear it again? You don't want to become His disciples, too, do you?"

28 They reviled him saying, "So, you are a disciple of that

---

blind?" Here we discover that the ban, or *cherem,* has already been placed on anyone who acknowledged Jesus as the Messiah, which meant being expelled from the community as well as being thrown out of the synagogue. It was forbidden to speak to anyone who was banned or to give him or her any type of comfort or aid.

24 They again call the man in to testify. This time the Pharisees invoke a solemn oath from Joshua 7:19. When Joshua charged Achan to tell the truth, he used this same oath. "Give glory to God!" they said. This is much the same as our promise in the courtroom to, "tell the truth, the whole truth, and nothing but the truth." Earlier Jesus made the point that God was to receive glory from the man's suffering. Here it is.

25 By now the man is tired of telling the story over and over. He reduces his experience to a sentence, which has described every follower's experience of Jesus since: "I was blind; now I see!"

26 Notice now that the Pharisees want to bring the discussion back to the subject of the making of the mud.

27 The man's response here cannot be anything else but humor.

28 The Pharisees' sense of humor leaves much to be desired. When they accuse the man of being a disciple of Jesus, their implication is that this was

(continued on next page)

man. We are disciples of Moses. **29** We know that God spoke to Moses. But this man, we do not even know where He comes from."

30 The man answered, "Now this is a remarkable thing indeed. You do not know where He comes from and yet He opened my eyes. **31** We know that God does not listen to sinners but if anyone fears God and does His will He hears that person. **32** It has never been heard of, opening the eyes of a man born blind. **33** If this man was not from God He would not be able to do anything."

34 They answered him, "You were born completely in sin, and you're teaching us?" So they banned him.

35 Jesus heard that the man had been banned from the synagogue. When He found him He said, "Do you believe in the Son of Man?"

36 The man answered, "And who is He, Sir, so that I might believe in Him?"

37 Jesus said to him, "You are now seeing Him and speaking with Him."

38 He said, "I believe, Lord." And so he worshiped Him.

---

all a hoax. They state, "We do not even know where He comes from." Yet in 7:52 they seem to know that He is from Galilee.

30 Whether from exhaustion or perhaps a newfound faith, the man has found the courage to speak his mind. He is openly amazed that these religious leaders have so little understanding of someone who has the obvious power that Jesus has.

34 Their statement, "You were born completely in sin, and you're teaching us?" was enough to have him "thrown out." This is not simply a physical act but the "ban" that was mentioned before. The man is now cast out of Jewish society. Even his parents are forbidden to speak with him. It is interesting that the Pharisees' conclusion about the man was an answer to the disciples' original question, "Who sinned?" though a wrong answer.

35 Jesus "found" him. This implies that He sought him out. He will still speak to the banned one, a further violation of their law.

36 You must realize that the man responds this way because he has never actually seen Jesus. Remember he was sent away to wash his eyes. When he left Jesus, he was still blind.

37 Poignantly, Jesus responds, "You are now seeing Him."

38 First, the man had his physical eyes opened. Now the eyes of his heart are opened as well. He makes the final step in his progression to faith by proclaiming Jesus as Lord.

39 Jesus said, "For judgment I came into this world so that those who cannot see might see and the ones who see might become blind."

40 The Pharisees who were with Him heard these things and said to Him, "We are not blind, are we?"

41 Jesus said to them, "If you were blind you would not have sin, but since you say 'we see,' your sin remains." ✖

H e sits there in his own personal darkness. John does not tell us his name because he could be any one of us, and is. He is begging because there is nothing else for a blind man to do in this culture, except starve. He cannot see, like so many others who have perfectly good eyes.

The disciples' discipling is not yet complete. They can still look at suffering and do nothing but talk objectively, theologically about it. After Jesus is done with them, they will be unable to see suffering without doing something about it.

The disciples' question, "Rabbi, who sinned, this man or his parents, that he was born blind?" comes from centuries of trying to understand the problem of suffering. Two thousand years later we still struggle and come up with the same kinds of ridiculous questions.

Beyond a misunderstanding of the cause and effect of sin, their question betrays a deeper ignorance of the nature of God. Through His actions and words Jesus will try to establish a fresh understanding of the Father. He will seek to open a door into a place where we are all invited to come and meet a Father who does not strike babies blind because they or their parents might have done something wrong. He will provide for us at last a redemptive way to

---

39   Jesus judges not as a judge but as the Light that accomplishes judgment. By its very nature, it illuminates and exposes.

40   For once Jesus is understood by the Pharisees. If a blind person, when offered a cure, insisted he was not blind, how could he ever be healed? Such persons render themselves incurable. Jesus' act of opening the eyes of the blind is really a parable of the deeper, more significant reality of who He is and what He means.

understand all our suffering, in the same light He understood all His suffering.

"His blindness," Jesus says, in effect, "is not a punishment but a possibility. This man is a waiting example of God's glory." His life is about to become a powerful parable.

Then comes the curious occurrence of Jesus spitting in the dirt, mixing the clay, and rubbing it on the man's blind eyes. So much has been said to try to explain this unusual action. The ancient sources list pages of medicinal uses for saliva, especially "fasting spittle," which, due to its connection to a righteous work, is particularly potent. Persius, Tacitus, and Pliny, the rabbis in the Mishna, all extol the uses of spittle. Could this be why Jesus utilizes it?

Others point to the symbolic activity of Jesus using dust, as it were, to recreate the man's eyes. John speaks of Jesus as Creator, after all, and here is one of His real-life examples of that truth.

Or perhaps Jesus' muddying the man's eyes forces an act of obedience and faith: He must go and wash at Siloam. This raises the blind man's expectations and gives him something to do in obedience to Jesus' command.

All of these explanations might be useful in helping us understand the miracle. However, a simple reading of the text is enough to point to the primary reason Jesus spat on the Sabbath. He was purposely breaking the Pharisees' oral law that forbade anyone to spit on the Sabbath lest the spit run down hill and make mud.

The first thing John says after the miracle is completed points to the offense. "The day on which Jesus *made the mud* . . . was a Sabbath." Amazingly, the making of the mud will become the central offense for which Jesus is condemned, not the healing.

Jesus purposely makes a public statement against the oral tradition, which the Pharisees had elevated to the same level of authority as the Bible.

The very act of sending the man off to a public place like Siloam to wash off the mud also tells us something. Jesus, who usually plays down the miraculous, often forbids the people He heals to even tell anyone about it. What kind of stir did He expect would result from sending the man to Siloam where, in the middle of the feast crowd, he would see for the first time in his life? Exactly the kind of commotion He got.

When his old friends ask how it happened, the man innocently tells them that Jesus made mud. Afterward he will always omit this detail from his testimony to the Pharisees because now he understands the difficulty this information will cause Jesus. When the "once-blind man" is brought in for questioning, he tells the Pharisees only that Jesus put mud on his eyes. He is silent about how the mud came to be made. Again and again they will ask him "how" he was made well. They want to hear more about the mud, not the miracle. Earlier the Jews asked for a miraculous sign from Jesus to prove He was who He claimed to be. Now that they have received this prophecy-fulfilling sign, they are unable to accept it because Jesus has broken their rules. People who ask for signs never believe them when they come. Jesus' actions unmask these people.

It is important to notice the progression in the faith of the blind man. His physical eyes were opened instantly beside the pool. His spiritual eyes open more gradually.

First he calls Jesus the "man," a good place for anyone to start understanding who Jesus is. Next, in the face of the interrogation of the Pharisees, he will say, "He must be a prophet," someone who speaks for God. Later, under further pressure, the man insists that if Jesus were not from God He could not heal someone blind from birth. This is a significant leap in understanding though it only involves a shift in one preposition. As the eyes of his heart begin to open, he sees that Jesus is from God.

The man takes his final step in coming to Christ in Jesus' presence, as we all must. After Jesus finds him in the crowd at the temple, He asks the harried man if he now believes in the Son of Man.

"Who is He?" the man asks, a question he had been forced to answer countless times since he had been healed.

"You are now seeing Him," Jesus says, "and speaking with Him."

At last, as his eyes come completely open, the man, who had never seen Jesus until now, confesses "I believe, Lord" and worships Him. It is his final step, and ours. Jesus explains the lived-out parable, which tells us why He has come: to give sight to the blind and to take away the sight of those who "see." It sounds harsh, and perhaps it is. For once the Pharisees understand clearly what Jesus means.

The disciples had asked if the man's physical blindness was a result of sin; the Pharisees later confirmed that the man was "steeped in sin at birth," just before they banned him from the synagogue. Now Jesus, the Light, causes the truth to shine.

The Pharisees had spoken more than they knew. Sin can cause blindness, only a blacker blindness than even they could understand. It is the Pharisees who are blind because of the sin of disbelief. Though they can see the beauty of creation, though they are able to witness the healing of a man born blind, they will not see. Theirs is a blindness that even Jesus, it seems, cannot heal.

JOHN 10

THE LORD IS MY SHEPHERD;
I SHALL NOT WANT.
PSALM 23:1

THE LORD IS
MY SHEPHERD

JOHN
10:1–42

1 "AMEN, AMEN, I say to you, the one who does not enter through the door of the sheepfold but goes up another way is a thief and robber. **2** But the one who enters through the door is a shepherd of the sheep. **3** The watchman opens up for him, and the sheep hear his voice. He calls his own sheep by name and leads them out. **4** When all of his own have come out, he goes on ahead of them. The sheep follow him because they know his voice. **5** They

---

The word of judgment at the closing of chapter 9 provides the context for the opening of chapter 10. The contrast will be made between false shepherds and the True Shepherd.

3 "Watchman" is a code word meaning the prophets (see Hab. 2; Ezek. 3; 1 Pet. 2:25; and Heb. 13:2).

5 The only time a sheep will not follow the shepherd is when it is sick.

will not follow a stranger but will run away from him because they do not recognize the voice of a stranger." **6** (Jesus told them this parable. But they did not understand the things He was saying to them.)

7 "AMEN, AMEN, I say to you," Jesus said, "I am the Door of the sheep. **8** All who came before Me were thieves and robbers, but the sheep did not listen to them. **9** I am the Door. If anyone enters through Me he will be saved. He will go in and out and find pasture.

10 "The thief comes only to steal, kill, and destroy. I have come so that they could have life and have it in abundance. **11** I am the Good Shepherd. The Good Shepherd lays down His life for the sheep. **12** The hired hand is not the shepherd who owns the sheep. When he sees the wolf coming, he leaves the sheep and flees. The wolf seizes the sheep and scatters them. **13** Because he is the hired hand the sheep do not matter to him. **14** I am the Good Shepherd. I know Mine, and Mine know Me. **15** Just as the Father knows Me and I know the Father and I lay down My life for the sheep.

16 "I have other sheep which are not of this fold. It is necessary that I bring these also. They will hear My voice, and they will become one flock with one Shepherd.

17 "This is why the Father loves Me, because I lay down My life that I might take it up again. **18** No one takes it from Me; I lay it down on My own. I have authority to lay it down and authority to receive it again. This command I received from My Father."

19 Again the Jews were divided because of these words.

---

7 Jesus alters the metaphor somewhat to help His listeners understand. When He calls himself the Door, He is still calling Himself the Shepherd since the shepherd would lie in the opening to the sheep pens in the fields, making himself the gate to keep the sheep safe from wandering away in the night.

11 For further insights, see Isaiah 40:11; Jeremiah 23:1–6; Ezekiel 34:11; and Zechariah 13:7.

13 This is a reference to the false shepherds mentioned in Zechariah 11:16.

19 Here we see an increased polarization of the crowd concerning Jesus.

20 Many of them were saying, "He has a demon," and "He is mad. Why do you listen to Him?"

21 Others said, "These are not the words of one who is demon possessed. A demon does not have the power to open the eyes of a blind man, does it?"

22 Then there was the Feast of Dedication in Jerusalem. It was winter **23** and Jesus was walking around on Solomon's porch in the temple.

24 The Jews encircled Him and said, "How long will You hold our souls in suspense? If You are the Christ, tell us plainly."

25 "I told you," Jesus answered them, "but you do not believe the works I do in My Father's name. They give witness about Me. **26** But you do not believe because you are not of My sheep. **27** My sheep hear My voice. I know them. They follow Me, **28** and I give them life eternal. They will never perish into the Age. No one will snatch them out of My hand. **29** My Father who has given them to Me is greater than all and no one has the power to snatch them out of the hand of the Father. **30** I and the Father are one."

22　It was winter. The Feast of Dedication commemorates the purification of the temple. In 164 B.C. Antiochious Epiphanies destroyed the temple, stole all the money from the treasury, and made it a capital offense to circumcise a child or even own a copy of the Torah. Mothers who were caught circumcising their baby boys were crucified with the infants hanging around their necks. Eight thousand Jews were killed. Swine flesh was offered to Zeus on the altar in the temple. It was the abomination Daniel had foreseen (see Dan. 11:31). The book of First Macabees records the struggle to retake the temple and reconsecrate it.

24　A two-month interval occurs between verses 21 and 22, time for the Jews' anticipation level to increase. This is a call from the people for Jesus to abandon the indirect communication that has characterized His ministry.

25　Much has led up to this statement from Jesus. So far every piece of evidence that pointed to His Messiahship has been denied by them.

27　Here is the connection, the discussion of Jesus as the Good Shepherd, that has brought John back to this place after two months. Here the most significant trait of the sheep is that they listen to the voice of their shepherd, something most of these people have been unwilling to do.

30　The Jews have asked for open communication from Jesus. When they receive it they pick up stones to kill Him. In the prologue John had said that the darkness could not comprehend the light.

31 Once again the Jews picked up stones to stone Him.

32 Jesus answered, "I have shown you many good works from the Father. For which one are you about to stone Me?"

33 The Jews answered, "We are not stoning You because of a good work but for blasphemy because You, a man, make Yourself out to be God."

34 "Has it not been written in your Law," Jesus answered, "'I said, You are gods?' **35** If He called them 'gods' to whom the word of God came, and the Scriptures cannot be undone, **36** then what about the One the Father set apart and sent into the world? Do you say He blasphemes because I said I am the Son of God? **37** If I do not do the works of the Father, do not believe Me. **38** But if I do, even if you do not believe in Me, believe the works that you may know and go on knowing that the Father is in Me and I in the Father."

39 They sought to seize Him again, but He slipped through their hands.

40 Jesus went away, back across the Jordan to the place where John was first baptizing. He stayed there **41** and many people came

---

32   The miracles signified that Jesus was God. Why should His verbal claim cause such a storm?

33   See Leviticus 24:16.

ᵂ34   Again Jesus quotes a psalm (82:6) and refers to it as the Law. The psalm He refers to is the shortest psalm of *Asaph,* one of the more insignificant psalmists. Yet in spite of this, Jesus accords the authority of the Law to the Wisdom writings. For John, who is basing the heart of his gospel on the Writings, this is a significant fact.

37   Again Jesus suggests the connection between the miracles and the claim.

40   Jesus had spent approximately eight months here at the beginning of His ministry (see John 3:22). Now He returns to where it all began to gain strength for the final confrontation. It is the calm before the final storm.

41   Notice this important detail: John had never performed a miraculous sign. To John's proclamation, Jesus added God's power. The statement from the people indicates that they believed John without the evidence of a miraculous sign; they had faith in the truest sense. Perhaps that is why they have followed Jesus into the wilderness. This group could be the core of believers He had come to establish.

to Him. They said, "Even though John never did a miraculous sign, everything John said about this man is true."

42 And in that place many believed in Him. 🎋

In Britain you still see them sometimes. They work alone or sometimes in pairs, always with a team of border collies nipping at the heels of their frightened and confused sheep. They are sheepherders, shepherds. The few I have come to know very well were manifestly patient men. You must be patient to work with sheep. "They are very dim," the English say.

When the Bible refers to us as sheep it is no compliment; they are not the brightest of God's creatures. The Sunday school picture of the shepherd leaning over the precipice to save a sheep with his crook is accurate. A sheep will literally follow its own nose off a cliff. Before sheep need food and water, sheep need a shepherd. And we, the Bible tells us, are just like that.

If this is true, then God knows we need a shepherd; so He sent us His Son, the Good Shepherd, to care for us, feed us, water, and protect us.

The adjective "good" implies that there are also bad shepherds. Jesus referred to them as "hired hands" who have no investment in the sheep. When trouble comes they run away. This would be bad enough, but the bad shepherds also kill the sheep, Jesus says. They care more about feeding themselves than feeding and caring for the sheep. The marks of a hired hand, or bad shepherd, then, are first cowardice and second, greed.

The Good Shepherd, as Jesus defines him, has two qualities. First of all, He knows the sheep. He calls each one by name. (The realization that we are known by name is manifestly comforting.)

The second trait of the Good Shepherd is that He is willing to lay down His life for the sheep as thoughtlessly as He lies down in the gap of the sheepfold at night, making Himself the door for the sheep. "This is why the Father loves Me," Jesus says. The Father gave to Jesus a special privilege that no one else has ever been given: the ability to let go of His life the way we might let go of a rope that is holding us up. On the cross Jesus does not succumb to blood loss or asphyxiation; instead we are told He "dismissed His Spirit," exercising the special privilege the Father had given Him. On the cross He is both the Lamb of God who gives His life for the world and the Good Shepherd who lays down His life for the sheep.

The sheep have only one important trait, but it is the only one they need: They listen to the voice of the Shepherd. They are able to discern between His voice, which they follow, and the voice of the hired hand, from which they flee. Their inability to follow a stranger is the single asset that keeps them alive. No one could snatch them from His hand.

It is appropriate that at the end of the chapter we see Jesus, the Shepherd, alone in the wilderness with the little flock He had come to gather. Without the proof of a miraculous sign, one of His followers' simple statement—"Everything John said about this man is true"—tells us the quality of their belief in Jesus. They believed without seeing, without the proof of a miraculous sign.

"And in that place many believed in Him," is another way of saying that they, like sheep, heard and recognized His voice and could do nothing else but follow.

LET HIM GO

JOHN
11:1–44

1 There was a man who was sick named Lazarus from Bethany, the village of Mary and her sister, Martha. **2** (Mary was the one who anointed the Lord with perfume and wiped His feet with her hair. Lazarus, the sick man, was her brother.)

The raising of Lazarus is the climactic miracle in the Gospel of John. It leads Jesus eventually to the cross.

1   Bethany is still called "Azarîyeh," derived from "Lazarus," who will become a major character in the final days. He is present at the last anointing at the home of Simon, the leper. He is being talked about and is probably present at Jesus' final entry into Jerusalem. He is included in John's Gospel as the only other target for murder in the plot to kill Jesus. The disciples are not seen as a threat by the priests, but Lazarus, someone who experienced a form of resurrection, which the priests taught was not possible, is living evidence of Jesus' power.

2   Although John has not at this point told the story of Mary anointing Jesus' feet, he assumes we already know it from the other Gospels.

3 The sisters sent word to Him saying, "Lord, look; the one You're so fond of is sick."

4 When Jesus heard about this, He said, "This sickness will not end in death but in the glory of God, that the Son of God may be glorified through it."

5 Jesus loved Martha and her sister, Mary, and Lazarus, **6** but when He heard that he was sick He stayed where He was for two more days.

7 Afterward He said to the disciples, "Let's go back to Judea."

8 The disciples said, "Rabbi, the Jews there want to stone You. You want to go back?"

9 Jesus answered, "Aren't there twelve hours of daylight? If someone walks around in the daylight he doesn't stumble because he sees by the world's light. **10** But if someone tries to walk around during the nighttime he stumbles because the light is not in him."

11 After this He said to them, "Our friend Lazarus has gone to sleep, but I'm going to wake him up."

12 So the disciples said, "Lord, if he's sleeping that means he will get better." **13** (But Jesus was talking about his death. They thought He meant resting sleep.)

14 So Jesus told them straight out, "Lazarus died **15** and I rejoice for you that I was not there so that you may believe. Let's go to him."

---

4   Like the blind man in chapter 9, Jesus reasons that Lazarus' death is really for God's glory. We should view our own crises in this light.

6   The word *but* is of tremendous importance. Even though His friend was sick, Jesus scandalously stays where He is, assuring, it would seem, Lazarus' death. Thus Jesus fails to meet the expectations of Martha, Mary, and probably even Lazarus.

11   Jesus consistently uses the metaphor of sleep for death (see Mark 5:39). In Jesus, death has lost its awful power; now it is only another form of sleep from which we will wake up, like Lazarus, at the sound of His voice. (See also Acts 7:60, where Stephen's death is also referred to as sleep.)

ᴹ12   The Motif of Misunderstanding appears here. Jesus has spoken about death in terms of sleep. In a deeply spiritual sense, this is really all it is. But the disciples misunderstand and hear only superficially.

15   For Jesus, the belief of His disciples is literally more important than life and death.

16 Thomas, the one they nicknamed Didymus, said to his fellow disciples, "We might as well go, too, so we can die right along with Him."

17 When Jesus got there, He found out that Lazarus had already been in the tomb for four days. **18** Bethany was close to Jerusalem, only two miles away, **19** and many of the Jews had come to Martha and Mary to console them about their brother.

20 When Martha heard Jesus was coming, she went out to meet Him. But Mary sat in the house.

21 Martha said to Jesus, "Lord, if You had been here my brother would not have died. **22** But even now I know that whatever You ask God, God will give You."

23 Jesus said to her, "Your brother will rise again."

24 "Yes, of course. I know he will rise in the resurrection on the last day," Martha said.

25 "I am the Resurrection," Jesus said. "Even if he dies, the one who believes in Me will live. **26** And everyone who lives and believes in Me will never die into the age. Do you believe this?"

27 "Yes, Lord," she said. "I have come to believe that You are the Christ, the Son of God, who has come into the world."

28 Having said this she left and called her sister, Mary. She whispered, "The Teacher is here and calls you."

29 When Mary heard this, she got up quickly and came to Him.

---

17 On Jesus' arrival we discover why He waited until Lazarus had been in the grave for four days. Jewish beliefs said that the spirit of the deceased would hover over the body for three days, but after that amount of time the body would become so disfigured that the spirit would no longer recognize it and would depart. From this primitive point of view, resurrection after three days would be even more impossible. All of the other people Jesus raised from the dead had only just died. Lazarus' case is unique.

20 One testimony to the accuracy of Scripture is the consistency of the characters from book to book (see Luke 10:38–42). Martha was always in motion, impatient. Mary was usually still and always at Jesus' feet.

ᴹ**24** Martha takes Jesus' promise as only a word of comfort, the kind of thing the mourners at her house had been telling her. This is another example of the Motif of Misunderstanding.

25 In the face of all her suffering, confusion, and disappointment, the only answer Jesus gives Martha is Himself.

135

30 Now Jesus had not come into the village yet but was still at the place where Martha had met Him. **31** When the Jews who were with her in the house consoling her saw Mary quickly getting up and leaving, they followed her, assuming she was going to weep at the tomb.

32 Mary came to the place where Jesus was. When she saw Him, she fell at His feet saying, "Lord, if You had only been here, my brother would not have died."

33 When Jesus saw her crying and the Jews who had come with her crying, His spirit gave a deep sigh and He was upset. **34** He said, "Where have you placed him?"

"Lord, come and see," they said.

35 The tears rose quietly into Jesus' eyes.

36 The Jews said, "Look, He was very fond of him."

37 But some of them said, "Couldn't someone who opened the eyes of the blind have kept this man from dying?"

38 Again, deeply moved, Jesus came to the tomb. It was a cave, and a stone was lying across it.

39 Jesus said, "Lift the stone."

The sister of the one who had died, Martha, said, "Lord, he already smells; it's been four days."

31　Jewish mourning customs dictated that the family would go to the tomb as many times as possible for a prescribed period of time.

32　Mary always leads with her heart. Again we find her at Jesus' feet. Though her words are the same as Martha's, the tone must have been completely different.

33　The verb translated "deeply moved" is used in classical Greek to describe a horse snorting. Here, we can imagine that Jesus shudders or perhaps groans.

35　In the New Testament Jesus is seen weeping two times, and two different verbs are used in the incidents. Here *edakrisen* (based on the word *dakru,* meaning "tear") denotes weeping silently; the picture is of a tear falling down the cheek. In Luke 19:41, when Jesus weeps over Jerusalem, the word *klaio* (where our word *cry* comes from) is used. It denotes uncontrollable weeping.

39　Again John makes the point that Lazarus has been dead for four days. He has begun to rot, and coming to life again is an impossibility.

40 "Didn't I tell you that if you believed you would see the glory of God?" Jesus told her.

41 So they lifted the stone and Jesus lifted His eyes and said, "Father, thank You for hearing Me. **42** I know You always hear Me; I only said it for the sake of all these people standing around, so that they may believe You sent Me."

43 Having said this, He shouted very loudly, "Lazarus, come out!"

44 And the dead man came out. His feet and hands were bound with strips of burial linen, and a sweat cloth was wrapped around his face.

"Untie him," Jesus said. "Let him go." ✄

A *story from the past . . .*
We had been staying on the other side of the Jordan, keeping our heads low for the time being. It was good to come back to the place where it all began. I had ministered with the Baptist here, and now he was dead. The sound of the water reminded me of him sometimes; the muddy smell in the air would take me back to those days when we waited with John to see who God would send.

The runner from Bethany was out of breath. It was clear from the look on his face that he had come on serious business. He told us Lazarus was sick; some thought he might even be dying. Martha had sent the messenger to fetch Jesus.

Jesus did not look concerned. He seemed to believe that Lazarus was going to be all right. "This illness will not end in death, it's for God's glory," He said, looking down in the grass.

---

42   Jesus prays out loud for the benefit of the people. Even for Jesus, miracles are just answered prayers.

44   The dead man came out still wrapped up like a mummy. The grave-clothes are described in the same terms as those in Jesus' empty tomb. Linen strips are wrapped around the body and a *sudorian,* or sweat cloth, is tied around his face.

He didn't move from that spot for two days. He would not shut Himself off from the rest of us; He talked and taught and told stories. I began to wonder if perhaps it was Jesus who was sick.

After the two days, He said, rather nonchalantly, "Why don't we go back to Judea."

There was a chuckle amongst the Twelve. But then we could see that He was serious.

I said, "I thought we had come here to get away from Judea and the Jews who want to stone You there! Is it because of Lazarus?"

"He's asleep. I'm going to go and wake him up," He said.

"If he's sleeping, that's a sure sign he'll get well," James said. "Why risk coming out of hiding? Besides it's almost Passover, and they'll be looking for You."

"He's dead," Jesus said flatly. "Lazarus is dead, and I'm glad for it because this might be the only way you'll ever come to believe. Now get your things together; let's go to him."

Jesus had nicknamed Thomas "Twin" because they looked so much alike; only now they could not have been more unlike each other. "Come on," Thomas moaned. "Let's go and get killed with Him."

As we reached the outskirts of the village we heard that Lazarus had died four days earlier. We were too late. But Jesus did not seem at all upset when He heard the bad news. We stopped at a well just outside the village to wash up and fill our water skins. Jesus rested in the shade of a small tree.

We heard her nervous, out-of-breath cries as she came sprinting down the road. There were little clouds of dust in the air behind her where she had taken each stride.

Martha, in black from head to toe, came straight toward Jesus, never even looking at the rest of us. She stood in front of Him, catching her breath.

"Where were You?" she said, almost scoldingly. "If You had come when I sent for You, he would not be dead now."

Jesus hadn't got up, hadn't even looked up. "Your brother is going to rise again," He said. He sounded tired.

"Sure," she said, "on the last day, at the Resurrection."

Jesus looked up into her eyes. His gaze quieted Martha. "I am the Resurrection," He whispered with intensity. "He believed in Me, and even though he's dead, now he will live because whoever lives in Me and believes in Me will never die. What about you, Martha. Do you believe?"

She was taken aback. Martha, always so quick to speak, chose her words carefully. She wanted to convince Jesus that she meant what she said. "Yes, Lord," she said as a strange calmness came over her face. "I do believe You are the Christ, God's Son, who has come into the world."

She turned away, almost in a daze. I expected her to have grabbed His sleeve and dragged Him home with her. But she just left, without another word; she simply turned around and walked back toward her house.

We had gathered up our traveling bundles and were about to leave for the village when we saw another, smaller figure in black coming toward us. She was not running exactly, but she was not walking either. It was Mary, Martha's beautiful sister. A crowd was following her at a respectful distance.

As she reached Jesus she collapsed at His feet. It was as if she had held herself together as long as she could, and could have perhaps held on to her composure a little longer, only now the sight of Jesus finally caused her to let go. Through a flood of tears she sobbed into the dust at His feet, her head turning from side-to-side as she spoke. "Oh, Lord, if You had only been here, Lazarus would not be dead now."

Martha had brought out Jesus' sterner side; Mary moved Him to tears. He was not sobbing like the rest of them. Yet as He glanced back to tell us to follow, I could see the tears trailing down His face.

We followed the two of them to a ravine outside the village. At the far end I could see the tomb, a natural cave that someone had sealed up with a large circular stone.

"Lift the stone." Jesus looked back at no one in particular in the crowd. No one made a move.

"Jesus, there is a stench by now," Martha said, again speaking as if to correct the Master.

Jesus looked sternly toward us, blinking back the tears. Peter and I understood what to do. We counted one, two, three, and heaved the stone aside. As it came to rest on the ground beside the tomb, I could smell the rottenness inside. Martha had been right. I moved away, unsure of what was about to happen. But Peter stood close by the tomb, his eyes fixed on Jesus as if he knew what He was going to do.

Then Jesus shouted at the top of his lungs, "Lazarus, come out!"

We all looked at each other, puzzled. What sort of lesson was this? Jesus had spoken of the life, but how would shouting into a tomb teach us anything about life?

I saw Peter give a start as he peered into the shadows of the tomb. All at once he jumped back and began scrambling up the steep walls of the ravine as a figure stepped into the doorway. I could not see the face. I was not sure if I wanted to see the face. But I knew it must be Lazarus.

He was barely able to walk, so tightly had the linen strips been wound around his legs. Through the gauze that wrapped his face he looked up at Jesus. I could just make out his toothy smile.

After that day, Lazarus never left Jesus' side. He was with us at mealtime. He followed us into the city, even though he knew the Jews now wanted to kill him as well. He followed us like a puppy, like a lamb. He would laugh at the most inopportune moments.

How do you relate to a dead man come alive again? How was he supposed to relate to us?

From time to time I would see him off to the side, talking quietly with Jesus. They shared a secret that they kept to themselves; after all, they were friends.

Years later Lazarus finally died . . . again. I was at the funeral. Jesus wasn't. Some of us had wondered if Lazarus would go on living into the Age, but finally his heart, so strained and strange since his first death, stopped beating.

We had never known quite how to relate to Lazarus. He was almost a saint in our community. They later named the village after him.

Just before Lazarus slipped away for the second time he began to whisper. We gathered around the bed, trying to understand what he was saying, but we couldn't make any of it out. I think it was because he wasn't whispering to any of us, but to his old Confidant.

OUR PLACE

JOHN
11:45–57

45 Many of the Jews who had come to Mary saw what He did and believed in Him. **46** But some of them went to the Pharisees and told them about what Jesus did.

47 A council of the chief priests and Pharisees assembled together and said, "What are we doing? This man is performing many miraculous signs. **48** If we leave Him alone, everyone will eventually believe in Him, and then the Romans will come and take The Place as well as our nation."

49 One of them, Caiaphas, high priest that year, said, "You know nothing! **50** You don't understand that it is better for you that one man die for the people than the whole nation perish."

51 (He did not say this from himself, but since he was high priest that year, he had prophesied that Jesus was about to die on behalf of the nation, **52** and not just the nation but also the children of God who had been dispersed, that they might be gathered together and become one.)

53 From that day on they planned to kill Him.

54 Because of this, Jesus quit walking around in the open, among the Jews. Instead He left and went into the country close to the desert, to a city called Ephraim. He stayed there with His disciples.

45–50 Jesus' gift of life results in setting the wheels in motion that will result in His death.

51–53 Caiaphas makes an effort to fulfill his own prophecy.

54 Jesus now takes His third major retreat to the wilderness. He returns from His self-imposed exile only for the party at Bethany where He will be anointed for His burial.

55 Now the Jewish Passover was near. Many from the country went up to Jerusalem before Passover to ritually purify themselves. **56** As they stood around in the Temple, they were looking for Jesus and saying to each other, "What does it look like to you? He won't come to the feast, will He?"

57 The chief priests and Pharisees had issued orders that if anyone knew where He was they should reveal it so they could arrest Him. ✺

The great issue that divided the Sadducees and the Pharisees was the matter of the Resurrection. The Sadducees read nothing concerning a resurrection in the Torah, the only books they accepted. The Pharisees could find proof of it throughout their Bible, which included the Law as well as the Prophets. It took a greater issue to bring them together: Jesus.

The Sadducees, wealthy, aristocratic, and in control. The Pharisees, poor mostly, working class, back-to-the-Bible folk. Separately they had been fighting for control of the people. The Sadducees controlled the temple, worship, and sacrifice. The Pharisees seemed to have won the hearts of the people with their teaching about the coming of the Messiah.

When the crowd came in with the report about the raising of Lazarus, the two groups met together. What concerned them most was not the people, or even the particulars of Jesus, but the threat He posed to what they called *Ha Makom,* "The Place," their temple.

The Romans barely tolerated their unusual worship. Imperial policy changed with the wind. Lately, because of the uproar the Sejanus incident had caused, (Sejanus's treachery toward the Jews had been uncovered by Caesar, and he was executed) Roman hostility had eased up. The soldiers' standards had been long removed from outside the temple walls. Things were going too well to allow the Galilean Carpenter to come along and mess them up.

Caiaphas, an eighteen-year veteran as high priest, reminded them of the prophecy he himself had given at his investment ceremony. It would be better to lose one troublemaker than the temple, the people, and possibly even their status as a favored nation in the Empire.

Caiaphas had said more than even he knew. Jesus would die at their hands; that was certain. But His death would accomplish in reality what Caiaphas had prophesied only in deceit. His death would bring together the nation as well as the scattered children of God. Jesus' death would herd them up like sheep, would draw all men to Himself. "We are going to have to make this happen," Caiaphas shouted as he slammed his fist on the meeting table.

It was back into hiding for Jesus and the Twelve. They fled to Ephraim, about sixteen miles from Jerusalem. He had been hiding from kings all his life it seemed, running to the desert where it would be safe. But the time for hiding was about to come to an end.

JOHN 12

SAVE NOW, (HOSANNA), O LORD, . . .
BLESSED IS HE WHO COMES IN THE NAME
OF THE LORD!

PSALM 118:25*

A HOUSE-FILLING FRAGRANCE

JOHN
12:1-11

1 Six days before Passover, Jesus came to Bethany, the home of Lazarus whom He had raised from the dead. **2** They gave a dinner for Him there; Martha served, and Lazarus was one of those who reclined at the table with Him.

---

1 John places Jesus' arrival in Bethany six days before Passover, one day before the final entry into Jerusalem, approximately one month after the raising of Lazarus. The banquet was not necessarily on this day.

2–8 The accounts of Jesus being anointed by a woman in the Gospels offer differing details. Matthew 26 and Mark 14 mention only a "woman" at the house of Simon, the leper, in Bethany. In both, Jesus mentions that it

(continued on next page)

3 Then Mary took a pound of genuine spikenard perfume. It was very expensive. She anointed Jesus' feet and wiped them with her hair. And the house was filled with the fragrance of the perfume.

4 Judas Iscariot, one of His disciples, who was about to betray Him, said, **5** "Why wasn't this perfume sold? It's worth a year's wages. We could have given it to the poor." **6** (He said this not because the poor mattered to him but because he was a thief and was stealing what went into the money box.)

7 Jesus said, "Let her be. She may keep it for the day of My burial. **8** The poor will always be with you but you won't always have Me."

---

was for His "burial." In both accounts she anoints Jesus' head. In both accounts an objection is made by the "disciples" or simply "those present." In both incidents Jesus memorializes her gift.

Luke refers to her as a "sinful woman" in the home of a Pharisee. In Luke's account the incident occurs earlier in the ministry, and the Pharisees object to Jesus' allowing Himself to be touched by her. In Luke she wets His feet with her tears and dries them with her hair.

Matthew and Mark are clearly describing a single event. Luke presents a completely different occurrence. Is John describing the same incident as Matthew and Mark with new details or, as he often does, is he describing still another anointing?

As in the first two Gospels, John places the event in the town of Bethany. While Matthew is not specific as to the time, Mark points to two days before Passover. While John first mentions a time of six days before Passover, after the account in verse 12 he also tells us that the "next day" was Jesus' final entry into Jerusalem.

John is not clear as to the place of the party. He mentions Bethany, "where Lazarus lived," but this is not to say that the party was held in his home. The familiar sisters are there. Martha, as always, is up and on the move, and Mary, true to character, is at the feet of Jesus. This detail, it seems, can be reconciled with the first two Gospels. While Lazarus was there with his two sisters, the party might have been at a friend's house—Simon the leper, perhaps, another person who had been healed by Jesus.

A detail absent from John's account is the alabaster jar. Mark tells us she broke the jar. One would think that John, who remembers the detail that the "house was filled with the fragrance of the perfume," would have remembered the alabaster jar although his reference to the "expensive" perfume might also refer to the costly alabaster container. *(continued on next page)*

⁹ A great crowd of Jews knew Jesus was there, but they didn't only come because of Jesus, but also to see Lazarus, whom He raised from the dead. ¹⁰ So the chief priests took it under advisement that they should also kill Lazarus ¹¹ since many of the Jews were going off and believing in Jesus because of his account. ✺

A *story from the past . . .*
It is interesting how powerfully smells can stir the memory. The scent of a flower can take you back half a lifetime to your first love. The aroma of incense always returns me to the first time, as a young boy, I ever saw the temple. The smell of the sea still brings back my father to me, sometimes so profoundly that I weep.

Just this morning, as I passed by the village perfumer, the scent of nard drifted into my nostrils, and all at once I was there once more, at Simon's house, with the Master. A crowd of curiosity-seekers stood outside the door, craning their necks to see Jesus and also, interestingly enough, Lazarus, "the dead man." He had become

---

John remembers specifically that it was Judas who objected to the "waste." His objection is identical to the ones in the first two Gospels. Mark and John both mention that it was worth a year's wages.

All three accounts record the detail that Jesus saw the anointing as a preparation for His burial. While Jesus does defend her actions in John's account, there is no memorial spoken in her behalf as there is in Matthew 26:13. Only in John does Jesus quote the passage concerning the poor from Deuteronomy 15:11.

It seems best to propose that John is telling the same story as Matthew and Mark while providing new details, as he typically does. If this is true, then the most important new detail is that the woman, Mary, anointed not only His head, as in the first two accounts, but also His feet. She also wiped His feet with her hair as the sinful woman had done months earlier.

9–10 It is interesting to hear that Lazarus is still a source of curiosity. John tells us that people came also to gape at the "dead man" as well as to see Jesus. The chief priests decide that it might be best to kill Lazarus as well, thereby destroying the evidence of Jesus' most famous miracle. It is the Saducean priests who want Lazarus dead and not the equally desperate Pharisees, since the Sadducees did not believe in the possibility of resurrection.

quite a celebrity since he strolled out of his tomb a month earlier the way any man might leave an empty house.

Lazarus, who had always been shy, didn't like all the attention. I heard a stranger ask him, "Are you the Lazarus who died and was resurrected?" He only answered, "Why?"

Lazarus was leaning back on his elbow, next to Jesus.

Martha was hovering over us all, making certain the glasses were kept full, whether we wanted more or not. Mary seemed especially quiet that day, off to herself in the corner. I was reclining on Jesus' left, the place of the intimate friend. Lazarus was on His right, the place of the honored guest. He hadn't wanted the special place, but Jesus had made him sit there.

Jesus was making conversation, not speaking to the group but to individuals, one at a time. He must have said something that no one else except Mary heard. As I think back, I wonder if He said something about what was going to happen to Him in just a few days.

She got up slowly and left the room, almost in a dream. I only noticed her leaving because we were in the middle of the meal, and I thought it a strange time to be going. She was away long enough to have gone to her own house, which was just a few streets over. When she returned she was carrying a marble jar wrapped in a piece of purple linen. We could all see that she had been crying; she was sniffling as she walked over behind Jesus. His feet were extended behind Him, as He was reclining.

I heard the seal on the jar snap and looked in amazement as she poured the perfume on His feet, making a puddle on the floor mat. As the oil spilled out so did her tears, and she began to shudder, like a mourner at a funeral.

All at once, as if she had just realized what she had done, she took off the scarf that was covering her hair and began trying to clean up the mess she had made. As her dark hair fell loose on the floor she took it and began, still sobbing, to wipe His feet. She didn't know what to do; none of us knew what to do. We all looked on in silent amazement.

After an awkward silence, Judas, who minded all our finances, said, "Do you realize what that ointment was worth? Do you know how many poor, hungry people it could have fed?"

Jesus spoke in the tone He always used when speaking from the Scriptures: "There will always be poor in the land," He said, quoting Deuteronomy. Then His voice softened and He added, "but you won't always have Me." It was His first warning to us. Others would follow, all of which we ignored.

We sat in silence, with only the sound of Mary's sniffling in the background. The looks on the disciples' faces, the taste of the bread in my mouth, the feel of the cold stone floor on my feet, the sadness in the Master's face, all were stored inside the fragrance of the perfume that filled the house. And just today, standing in the middle of the busy marketplace, with tradesmen bartering and donkeys braying, I was lifted up and taken back in time to that sad moment, and all by the smell of that perfume. I wept along with Mary.

A Tearful Entry

JOHN
12:12–19

12 On the next day the great crowd that had come to the feast heard that Jesus was coming to Jerusalem. **13** They took the branches of palm trees and went out to meet Him. They were shouting, "Hosanna! Blessings on the One who comes in the name of the Lord and King of Israel!" **14** Jesus found a young donkey and sat on it, just as it was written,

> **15** "No fear, Daughter of Zion
> Look! your King is coming
> Sitting on the foal of a donkey."

---

12   John describes the crowd as "great." This might be an understatement. The population of Jerusalem, normally about 50,000, swelled to 250,000 during Passover in Jesus' day.

13   It is important to note that the crowd, waving palm branches, is from Jericho, "the city of the palms." This is not the same group that will shout for Jesus' crucifixion in a week's time. That "mob" would be composed of the rabble of Jerusalem, of men who were susceptible to the coercion of the high priest.

The crowd is cheering because Jesus has just recently healed a man born blind at Jericho. John will later mention that Lazarus' story is still much on people's lips, much to the chagrin of the Pharisees.

"Blessed is he . . ." is a common Passover greeting from Psalm 118.

14–15   The riding of the colt, in fulfillment of Zechariah 9:9, is full of meaning. The prophetic passage mentions the breaking of the war bow; it is about the coming of a king in peace. Jesus' mount signified that He was coming to make an end of hostilities—not just between Jews and Gentiles but between God and humanity.

16 At first the disciples did not understand these things, but when Jesus was glorified they remembered that these things had been written about Him and that they had done these things to Him. **17** The crowd that had been with Him when He called Lazarus out of the tomb and raised him from the dead were giving their testimonies. **18** Because they heard that He had done this sign, the crowd went out to meet Him. **19** The priests said to one another, "See, nothing has been gained. Look, the world has gone after Him." 🎔

Whenever a city was conquered in the ancient world, the type of animal the victorious king would ride as he entered a defeated town would make all the difference in the world to the people. If he was seated on a horse, the city was doomed; it was a sign that he had come in war, riding his "warhorse." If he was riding a donkey everyone would breathe a sigh of relief because this was a sign that he was coming in peace. (It is difficult to fight a battle riding a little donkey!)

This helps us understand why Zechariah said, "Do not be afraid, Daughter of Zion. Your king is coming on the foal of a donkey." Riding a donkey is a sign of peace. The king has not come to conquer but to forgive, so don't be afraid.

The rabbis taught if Israel was not ready when the Messiah came He would ride the foal of a donkey, but if she was ready, He would ride a white horse. The Synoptics tell us that Jesus went to great lengths to make sure He had a donkey's foal on which to enter Jerusalem; He sent His disciples ahead into town to fetch one.

It was John's privilege to witness both "comings" of the Messiah. Here, at the final entrance into Jerusalem, he is there, helping to guide the confused animal through the noisy crowd as the "King of Israel" comes in peace. Jesus had said earlier, "I have not come to judge but to save." Now, riding the foal, He enters Jerusalem to do just that.

ᴅ**16**   Again we see John's unique, backward-looking perspective. It is not until later on that the disciples realized the significance of the things they had done on the arrival of Jesus. John tells us now of their later realization.

Later, after his account of Jesus' life had been written, John witnessed the second and final Coming of the Messiah, by way of a vision. He had just gotten up after falling to his knees to mistakenly worship an angel. As he looked up he saw heaven open and before him, he saw Someone he recognized, this time riding a white horse. Jesus had come to make war against the kings of the earth and the beast (Rev. 19:11).

They could not seem more different, the suffering Servant on the donkey that day, His feet dragging the ground, wiping away the tears He had just been weeping for Jerusalem, and the resplendent Warrior-King, eyes blazing like fire with many crowns adorning His head. Yet John recognizes both as his beloved Friend.

THE GREAT
TURNING POINT

JOHN
12:20–26

20 There were some Gentiles among those who were going up to worship at the feast. **21** They approached Philip of Bethsaida of Galilee and asked him, "Sir, we want to see Jesus."

22 Philip went and told Andrew, then Andrew and Philip told Jesus.

23 Jesus answered, "The hour has come for the Son of Man to be glorified.

24 "AMEN, AMEN, I say to you, unless the grain of wheat which falls into the ground dies, it remains alone. But if it dies it bears much fruit. **25** Whoever cherishes his life loses it. But the one

---

20   The "coming of the Greeks," a seemingly insignificant occurrence in the flow of the narrative, marks a major event in the ministry and mind of Jesus. John had substituted the second temple expulsion with this incident. He knows we have heard about the second ruckus in the temple, but we do not know about the Gentile "God-fearers" who came to Jesus as a result of His actions on their behalf. The Greeks have come because they see in Jesus Someone who cared so much about their having a place in the temple to pray that He risked His life, confronting the priests in general and the powerful Annas in particular.

21   They come to Philip presumably because he has a Greek name.

23   Again Jesus sees the suffering before Him as being tied up with glory, a perspective we still find difficult to grasp. His beautiful pronouncement, like a soliloquy, speaks of the principle of the Cross as it is seen in nature; death is always a necessity for new life. This truth, the truth of Jesus' life, was woven into the fabric of our world.

who hates his life in this world will keep it into life eternal. If anyone serves Me, let him follow Me, and where I am, My servant will be also. **26** If anyone serves Me, the Father will honor him." ❧

Although John does not record the second temple expulsion, he does give us one of the immediate results of it, the coming of the Gentile "god-fearers" to see Jesus. It is only natural that, having witnessed what He did on their behalf in the temple, some of the Gentile believers would want to see Jesus, perhaps only to thank Him for fighting so fiercely to make their place in the temple once more a place of prayer.

It seems an innocent enough incident, but it brings about a profound reaction in Jesus. All through the Gospel it has been said again and again, "His hour had not yet come." The phrase is used to explain why no one could apprehend Jesus, though many tried. Jesus used the phrase to try to stay out of the goings-on at Cana. Each time we read the phrase in the Gospel it always seemed to imply that a time was coming for Jesus. Now that time has indeed come, and the coming of the Gentiles is the sign Jesus has been waiting for.

The Jews have consistently refused to believe. Even those who supposedly believed demanded signs as proof, something Jesus was loathe to do. "He came to that which was His own," John told us in the prologue, "and His own would not receive Him." But now the "other sheep" Jesus spoke of are here, waiting to enter into the fold through Him. The time has come for the Shepherd to lay down His life for all the sheep. The Greeks have come as the firstfruits of the great harvest that will result from the grain of wheat, Jesus Himself, falling into the ground to die.

---

25 Jesus does not promise a trouble-free existence for the disciple; rather He promises to always be with us.

THE VOICE

JOHN
12:27-36

27 "My soul is troubled now. What can I say? Father save Me from this hour? It was for this hour that I came. **28** Father, glorify Your name."

A voice came out of heaven, "I have glorified it and will glorify it again."

29 The crowd that was standing there and heard it said, "It just thundered!"

Others said, "An angel has spoken to Him."

30 Jesus answered, "This voice did not come for Me but for you. **31** Now is the judgment of this world. Now the ruler of this world will be cast out. **32** But I, if I am lifted up [crucified] above the earth, I will draw all people to Myself." **33** (He said this to make clear the way He would die.)

ᴹ**28–31**   Here is the Motif of Misunderstanding, a much-neglected audition of God in the New Testament. The voice that seems to comfort Jesus in His hour of turmoil is, for those who were standing by, mistaken for the sound of thunder rumbling or perhaps an angel's voice. God's own voice from heaven is misunderstood.

32   This is one of the most misquoted verses in the New Testament. The meaning of the metaphor "lifted up" is often confused for praise and not crucifixion. So the misunderstanding has grown that Jesus said that the simple act of praising Him would draw the world to Him. It is not the intent of the verse. The context is the coming of the Greeks. The "world" is represented by their coming. The Jews have rejected Jesus and will go on to fully say no to Him. The next verse seals this understanding. Jesus said "lifted up" to indicate that He would be crucified, that is, nailed to a high Roman cross.

34 The crowd answered Him, "We heard from the Law that the Christ will be with us forever. What do You mean when You say that the Son of Man must be crucified? Who is this One You call the Son of Man?"

35 Jesus said to them, "The Light is with you only a little time yet. Walk while the Light is with you or else the darkness might overtake you. Whoever walks in the darkness does not know
where he is going. 36 While you have the Light, walk in the Light.
Then you will be sons and daughters of the Light."

Jesus said these things and then left and hid from them.

His words sound almost like a Shakespearean tragedy: "Now is My soul troubled. And what shall I say? . . ." He could almost be Lear, standing on the heath, the storm gathering behind Him, with the knowledge that the "poor, naked wretch," was soon to be Him.

"What shall I say? Father save Me from this hour?" Jesus asks. It is the seed of a tormenting question that will flower in the blackness of Gethsemane, where Jesus will ask the excruciating question again.

"No," He tells Himself then. This is why He has come. "Father, glorify Your name." This is the great hope to which Jesus clings. Not His own rescue, but the thought that the name of the One who sent Him would be glorified through the ordeal He was about to suffer. He has talked about bringing glory to His Father before. Now, as the magnitude of the cost of that glory looms

---

34 The crowd also clearly understands "lifted up" as a reference to Jesus' death.

w35 In answer to their question, "Will Christ abide forever?" Yes, the Christ will abide forever, but like the Light, He will not always be visible (see Luke 17:22; John 7:34; and Matt. 21:43). Their reference to the Law is in fact from Psalm 110 and the person called Melchizedek, a Messianic figure. Jesus will consistently refer to Wisdom passages as the Law.

By saying "Whoever walks in the darkness . . ." Jesus refers to Proverbs 4:19.

36 Jesus returns to the village in secret.

before Him, the Father speaks from heaven. It is the most neglected audition of God in the New Testament.

God does not say, "It's almost over," or "You will be with Me soon." He gives His Son the comfort He wants and needs most to hear: "I have glorified it and will glorify it again."

The voice sounded to some like thunder, their ears unable to hear anything but the roar of it. To others, perhaps more used to listening for the voice of God, it sounded like an angel. Their differing responses to the voice separate them into the scientific and the superstitious. None of them was able, it seems, to understand the words of the voice. This has been their consistent condition throughout the Gospel of John. They do not hear at all, and if they do hear, they misunderstand.

Jesus tells the confused crowd that the voice has not spoken for Him but for the sake of the people. Before, when He "woke up" Lazarus, Jesus told the Father that He was speaking out loud for the sake of the people and not the Father, who always hears. It is hard not to believe, though, that the Father was speaking, in some small way, to comfort His Son.

The judgment of the world is about to occur, Jesus says, meaning that the penalty for the world's sin is about to come crashing down upon Him. The world would be punished through His own body on the tree. And so the world, and no one else in the world, would ever be the same.

Before the cross of Jesus, the opposite of sin was being good, and the world bumbled along trying to be good enough, hoping to escape the judgment. Now the judgment of the world would fall on Jesus, who alone had been good, perfectly good. The rules would now forever change. The opposite of sin would become faith in Jesus, not righteousness by works. If we are condemned it will not be for our sin, which He has already paid for, but for refusing to have faith in Him. The opposite of sin has become faith in Christ!

"If I am lifted up (crucified) above the earth, I will draw all people to Myself," He says, making crystal clear that a cross is waiting for Him. "Lifted up" is the consistent phrase used in John to describe crucifixion. It does not mean praise. Jesus never implied that praising Him would draw all men, but rather we would be

159

drawn to Him by His sacrifice, wherein the need we all share for forgiveness would be satisfied.

The people understand perfectly that Jesus is talking about death on a cross. But if the Law says Christ will live forever, how could He be crucified? they ask. They want more clarification about who this "Son of Man" is. But the time for discussion is over. For the second time Jesus warns them that He is not going to be with them much longer. His Light will not be visible for long.

WHAT ISAIAH SAID AND SAW

JOHN
12:37–50

37 Even though He had done so many miraculous signs in front of them, they did not believe in Him. **38** This happened so that the prophet Isaiah's word would be fulfilled:

"Lord, who has believed what we said?
And to whom has the power of the Lord been revealed?"

39 Therefore, they did not have the power to believe because as Isaiah also said:

40 "He has blinded their eyes
and hardened their hearts
So that they cannot see with their eyes
And understand with the heart
And turn and be cured."

41 Isaiah said these things because he saw His glory and spoke about Him. **42** Nevertheless, even some of those in leadership believed in Him but because of the Pharisees they were not confessing it openly because they might be banned from the synagogue. **43** This is because they loved the glory of men more than the glory of God.

44 Jesus shouted, "Whoever believes in Me, not only believes in Me but in the One who sent Me. **45** And whoever sees Me sees the One who sent Me. **46** I, the Light, have come into the world so that everyone who believes in Me does not have to stay in the darkness.

47 "If anyone hears My words and does not keep them I do not judge him. I did not come to judge the world but to save it.

48 "Whoever dismisses Me and My words has a judge, the Word I spoke; it will judge them on the last day. **49** I do not speak of Myself but for the One who sent Me. The Father who sent Me has given Me a command, telling Me what to say. **50** I know His command is life eternal. Therefore, the things I say are just what the Father has said to Me." ❧

It is a sad but amazing fact that those who demand miraculous signs never believe them when they come. That is John's point as the public ministry of Jesus comes to an end. Jesus' witness to the people has been consistent. He has perfectly fulfilled every sign the prophets had ever spoken. He has preached, begging them to open their eyes, but the response has been persistent disbelief and willful misunderstanding.

John quotes a passage in Isaiah that was written in an identical context. The prophet had reached out to the people through his preaching again and again, and yet they refused to listen. It is important to understand this context to avoid misunderstanding the tone of the quote. It is the basis of an idea that is woven through the New Testament, where it is quoted five times:

> Who has believed our message?
> To whom has the powerful arm of the Lord been
> revealed?

Perhaps the second question should be, "To whom *hasn't* the power of the Lord been revealed?" Everyone has seen His power in creation, Paul says, and is responsible for what he or she has witnessed; these people are without excuse (see Rom. 1:19).

---

49 The reference is to Deuteronomy 18 and "the Prophet like Moses." This statement is an appropriate closing to the public ministry of Jesus.

A dead man has walked out of a tomb and stands there beside Jesus, but still they will not see and understand who has come to them. God's own voice is still echoing in the distance, and they discuss whether or not it was thunder. And now the Light is about to leave. He came to open their eyes, but they were unwilling to wash off the clay.

Jesus' last words, like so many of His previous words, are spoken as the Prophet. Like Moses, He has only spoken the words the Father has given Him to speak. They are the final shot in the battle that was His life.

"I have said just what the Father told me to say." He could do nothing more for them now but die.

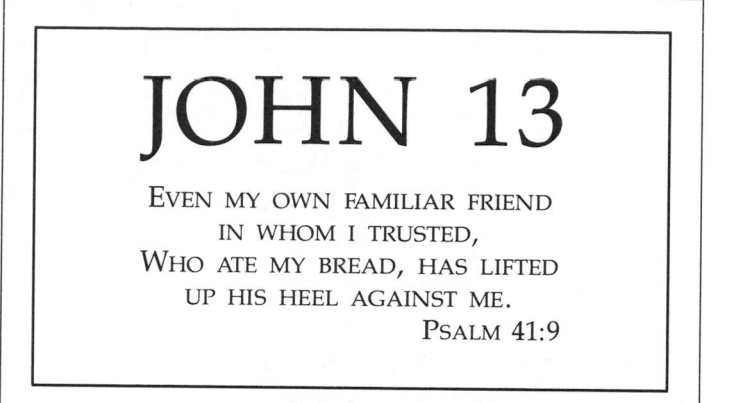

JOHN 13

EVEN MY OWN FAMILIAR FRIEND
IN WHOM I TRUSTED,
WHO ATE MY BREAD, HAS LIFTED
UP HIS HEEL AGAINST ME.

PSALM 41:9

HOW MUCH SMALL THINGS CAN SHOW

JOHN
13:1–17

¹ Before the Passover feast, Jesus knew His hour had come to pass from this world to the Father. To the ones He loved in this world, He now showed the full extent of His love.

² During supper, the devil having already put into the heart

Even as John, in chapter 12, substituted the coming of the Greeks in his narrative at the point where the Synoptics place the second temple expulsion, so now the footwashing is substituted at the point where the other Gospels place the Last Supper.

2 Judas formed the plot six days earlier at Simon the Leper's house (see Matt. 26:14). Note that the devil prompted, but Judas acted.

of Judas, son of Simon Iscariot, that he would betray Him, **3** knowing that the Father had placed all things into His hands and that He came from God and was returning to God, **4** He got up from supper and took off His outer robe. Taking a linen towel, He wrapped it around Himself. **5** Then He put water into a wash basin and began to wash the feet of the disciples, wiping them dry with the towel He had wrapped around Himself.

6 He came to Simon Peter, who said to Him, "Lord, are You really going to wash my feet?"

7 Jesus answered, "You cannot understand what I am doing now, but after these things you will understand."

8 Peter said, "Never, ever will I allow You to wash my feet."

Jesus answered, "Unless I wash you, you have no share with Me."

9 So Simon Peter said to Him, "Lord, then not only my feet but also my hands and my head."

10 "The one who has already bathed is clean," Jesus said, "he only needs to wash his feet. You are clean, but not all of you." **11** (He knew who was going to betray Him. That is why He said, "Not all of you are clean.")

12 After He had washed their feet and put on His robe, He reclined once more and said to them, "Do you have any idea what I have just done for you? **13** You call me Teacher and the Lord; well

---

3 The context for the footwashing must be recovered from Luke 22:24, where we read that the disciples were caught up again in the argument over who would be the greatest. Jesus' actions are a response to this argument.

4 Jesus, aware that the Father had put everything under His power and that He was returning to God, does not respond as we might expect but rather takes up the towel to perform the task of the most lowly slave, a task John the Baptist had earlier stated he was not worthy to perform for Jesus.

7 Jesus emphasizes to Peter that even though he does not understand now, later he will by the Spirit (see John 12:16).

8 Peter too frequently puts together these two words, "No" and "Lord." The Greek is emphatic: "You will never *ever* wash my feet."

9 Peter quickly forgot his previous emphatic statement.

10 They are clean because of the Word (see John 15:3).

12 Jesus asks a question and does not wait for an answer.

said, for I am. **14** So if I wash your feet, I who am your Lord and Teacher, you should also wash each other's feet. **15** I just gave you an example. What I just did, you also should do.

16 "AMEN, AMEN, I say to you, a servant is not greater than his lord, nor the one sent greater than the one who sent him. **17** If you know these things, you will be blessed if you do them." ✻

Mother Teresa of Calcutta encourages her followers to do "small things for God." She teaches that through a simple act, like offering a cup of water or even simply giving someone a smile, we can fully demonstrate God's love.

When, at the end of His earthly ministry, Jesus wanted to show "the full extent of His love" He did so by the simple act of washing the feet of His disciples. It was indeed an earthshaking event for the Lord of the universe, who knew that all authority had been placed into His hands, to use those same hands to wash the disciples' dirty feet. The very simplicity of Jesus' act has given it the power to capture the imaginations of His followers for two thousand years.

The Synoptics tell us that the disciples had been arguing about who would be the greatest. Perhaps their bickering had become more than Jesus could bear. He interrupted the meal in what must have seemed to the disciples a bizarre way. He has finally given up on words and decides to enact a parable of servanthood.

The consistency of the individual characters throughout the Bible is one of the great proofs of its accuracy. Peter is always himself, no matter which Gospel you choose. When Jesus came to him, the old hardhead put together an impossible combination of two words, "No" and "Lord." His persistent impetuousness caused him to flip-flop from refusing to let Jesus touch his feet to asking to be given a bath. Many times our attitudes, like Peter's, say, "You will never wash my feet." Yet, Jesus says, a heart that humbly

---

14–16 Jesus makes a frontal assault on the subject of their quarreling about who was the greatest.

accepts His humble ministering is the only heart that has a part in Him.

You can tell that time is getting short by Jesus' almost desperate question to the disciples: "Do you understand what I have just done for you?" Never in the Gospel has He asked such a pointed question. But now it is getting late, and they need to comprehend this, of all lessons. "I just gave you an example," He tells them. He wants this pattern of servanthood to become the pattern of their lives. The earlier discussion concerning who was greatest, a discussion they seemed to have frequently had, is no longer appropriate. Jesus makes clear that His call is to radical servanthood. And so, even as His actions validated everything else He has said, He now demonstrates what He means by His powerful example.

After the Resurrection Jesus will again be their Servant as He prepares their breakfast on the shore of the lake (see John 21). Later still, Jesus promised them He would again get up from the table at the great Messianic feast, change into the clothes of a servant, and wait on those who had been His faithful servants (see Luke 12:37). But for now He shows them the full extent of His infinite love by doing something small, by washing their feet.

THE INTIMATE FRIEND

JOHN
13:18–33

18 "I am not talking about all of you. I know whom I have chosen. But so the Writings may be fulfilled, 'The one who eats My bread has lifted up his heel against Me.' **19** I have told you all this before it happened so that when it happens, you will believe I am.

20 "AMEN, AMEN, I say to you, whoever receives the one I send receives Me. And whoever receives Me receives the One who sent Me."

21 After He had said these things Jesus was troubled in spirit. He gave witness saying, "AMEN, AMEN, I say to you, one of you is going to betray Me."

22 The disciples looked at each other, not knowing which one He was talking about. **23** One of the disciples was reclining close to Jesus; it was the one He loved. **24** Simon Peter nodded to him to ask who it was that Jesus was referring to.

ᵂ18 The hints of Judas's guilt are piling up to the point that when he does finally betray Jesus no one expresses surprise. Again, it is significant that Judas's betrayal is viewed through a passage from the Wisdom literature.

20 Note again "the One who sent Me," Jesus' favorite circumlocution for the Father. Jesus is the "sent One."

ᴰ22 John records the detail that at the moment of Jesus' pronouncement of betrayal the disciples "looked at each other." This is the exact moment depicted in da Vinci's painting of the Last Supper.

23 John is reclining next to Jesus. He will later use this detail to identify himself (see John 21:20). He is close enough to whisper in His ear.

25 He leaned back against Jesus and said, "Lord, who is it?"

26 Jesus answered, "It is the one who will take the morsel I have dipped when I give it to him."

He dipped the morsel and gave it to Judas, son of Simon Iscariot.

27 After the morsel, Satan entered him.

Jesus said to him, "Hurry up and do what you are about to do."

28 None of the ones reclining knew why He spoke to him. Some thought that, **29** because Judas had the money box, Jesus was telling him to buy what they needed for the feast, or that he might give something to the poor. **30** As soon as he took the morsel, that man left. And it was night.

31 After he went out, Jesus said, "Now the Son of Man is glorified. **32** And God is glorified in Him. If God is glorified in Him, God will glorify Him in Himself, will glorify Himself immediately.

33 "Little children, I am only with you a little while longer. You will look for Me. I will tell you what I told the Jews, where I am going you do not have the power to come." ❧

Six days earlier Judas Iscariot had gone to the high priests and asked, "What will you give me if I hand Him over to you?" (Matt. 26:15). He is no helpless pawn, as the "Jesus" movies usually portray him. We usually give Judas the benefit of the doubt because we would like to give ourselves the same benefit. Yet there is no doubting the character of the one whose name disappears in the narratives at this point and becomes simply, "The one who betrayed Him."

---

25 John leans back against Jesus to ask Him the question. If they are leaning on their left elbows this would indicate that John is sitting on the right side of Jesus. If Judas can dip his bread in the same cup as Jesus, he must be on His left. In Semitic culture the left hand was the place of the intimate friend. This would add even more detail to the prophecy in Psalm 41:9 regarding the intimate friend.

29 Because the disciples assume that Judas is going to give money to the poor we can gather that it was their regular custom to do this. In John

(continued on next page)

It is significant that Jesus used a passage from the Wisdom writings to explain who Judas really was. Psalm 41 describes this person as "my own familiar (or intimate) friend." Some believe, on account of this passage, that Judas may have been one of Jesus' closest friends until the betrayal. Later Gospel writers would have erased any references to their friendship in light of the final betrayal. In the psalm, the "friend" is said to have "lifted up his heel," a metaphor of betrayal. When David wrote these words could he have possibly imagined that the betraying friend would lift up his heel so that it might be washed by the One he would betray?

Trying our best to reconstruct the seating arrangement at the table, we can speculate that John, reclining and leaning with his back against Jesus, is on Jesus' right. This was known, even as it is today, as the place of honor. Judas, it seems, is on Jesus' left, close enough for Jesus to whisper to him. He is within reach of Jesus, who gives him the ceremonial sop of bread and bitter herbs. If this speculation is correct it would also support the psalm's description, since the left hand, in the ancient world, was known as the place of the "intimate friend."

After handing him the sop, Jesus tells Judas to hurry up and finish the work he has already started. As Judas leaves, no one seems suspicious of him. They suppose he is going to buy provisions or perhaps give money to the poor, a ritual observance during Passover. (The rabbis taught that giving to the poor was as important as studying the Law.) Had they known what he was about to do, Judas would have never left the room alive. But the dark man goes out into the dark night, taking a measure of darkness with him.

We might have expected Jesus to say anything other than what He did say after Judas left, perhaps, "Now is the Son of Man betrayed. Now is the Son of Man about to be arrested." But of all

---

12:5 Judas complained about the waste of the oil that might have been given to the poor. It is interesting that the very one who betrayed Jesus was responsible among the Twelve for giving to the poor. A counterfeit social concern often masks a lack of faith in Jesus.

30   Judas's departure ushers in the night that Jesus had mentioned before (see John 12:35). The Light would soon be going.

33   This form, "little children," is found only here and in 1 John.

things, Jesus says, "Now the Son of Man is glorified." It is as if Judas's departure set in motion once and for all the order of events that would bring Jesus finally to the cross and to glory. The next time Jesus will see Judas, he will be at the head of a detachment of soldiers. Never forget, however, that just before that, Jesus had washed his feet and placed him in the place of the intimate friend.

COMMAND VS. COMMANDMENT

JOHN
13:34–38

34 "A new command I give to you: Love one another. As I have loved you, love one another. **35** Everyone will know by this that you are My disciples, if you have love amongst yourselves."

36 Simon Peter said to Him, "Lord, where are You going?"

"You do not have the power to go where I am going," Jesus answered, "but you will follow later."

37 Peter said to Him, "Why can't I follow You right now? After all, I am willing to lay down my life for You."

38 Jesus answered, "You will lay down your life for Me? AMEN, AMEN, I say to you, the dawn will not break until you deny Me three times." 🦋

Jesus called them His "little children." Certainly they had acted like children that night, but that is not what Jesus meant. The point is He loves them like little children. And now He issues the command to love. The only distinguishing characteristic for His disciples from now on will be their ability to love the way their Master loves.

---

35 The only distinguishing mark of the disciples ever given in Scripture is their ability to love.

ᴹ36 Simon Peter has failed to hear the command to love and asks instead about Jesus' earlier statement that He is soon going somewhere (see v. 33). This is an example of the Motif of Misunderstanding.

How could anyone issue a commandment that could force people to love each other? To fully understand what Jesus meant we must note the subtle difference between a command and a commandment.

A commandment, or law, is only written for those who are lawbreakers. Those who keep the law do not need laws. The breaking of a commandment brings a prescribed penalty. The guilty must be punished; that is the heart of the power of laws.

The heart of a command is love and obedience. A command is entrusted to obedient servants. It carries with it a blessing; that is the heart of its power. The motivating force of the law is fear. The law implies judges and executioners; the command points only to the Lord who speaks it.

If you break a law, you are guilty and subject to punishment. If you disobey a command, you are disobedient and are left standing in the presence of a Lord who is disappointed.

This subtle difference provides a more powerful encouragement to obedience than the fear of the law could ever hope to give. Those who try to change Jesus' commands into commandments completely destroy their character and render following Him impossible.

Peter's question reveals that he had stopped listening when Jesus told them He was going somewhere they could not follow. The new command would have to wait to be impressed on Peter's heart when the Spirit would remind him of it. Peter only heard that Jesus was going to a place he could not follow, and this upset him. He seems to have an intimation of Jesus' impending death because he swears his allegiance even to death.

The disciples seem to have returned to their earlier argument about who was the greatest. Nothing else could explain the pronouncement of Jesus' crushing prediction that Peter would deny Him before sunup. Could Peter have misunderstood and assumed that he was the betrayer that Jesus had earlier spoken about? No doubt, Peter means what he says when he pledges to die with Jesus. The problem is, he doesn't know the real meaning of what he said, for in a matter of hours Jesus will be dead and Peter in hiding.

THE WAY,
THE TRUTH,
THE LIFE

JOHN
14:1–14

¹ "Do not let your hearts be troubled. You believe in God, believe in Me as well. ² In My Father's house are many places to stay. If it were not so, I wouldn't have told you that I am going to prepare a place for you, would I? ³ And if I go and prepare a

---

Chapter 14 represents the discourse at the table after the Last Supper.

1 The context for verse 1 is provided by the final verse of the previous chapter: Jesus has just spoken of betrayal.

2 The Greek word translated "room" is from the word *monai*, from *meno*, meaning "to stay." The idea is not of specific rooms but of places to stay, places prepared just for us.

place for you that means I will come back to gather you together so we can all be together. **4** You know the way to the place I am going."

5 Thomas said to him, "Lord, we do not know where You are going, so how would we be able to know the way?"

6 "I am the Way and the Truth and the Life," Jesus said. "No one comes to the Father except through Me. **7** If you know Me, you also know My Father. From now on, you do know Him and have seen Him."

8 Philip said to Him, "Lord, then show us the Father; that will be enough."

9 "I have been with you so long, Philip," Jesus said, "and still you do not know Me? The one who has seen Me has seen the Father. How can you say, 'Show us the Father?' **10** Do you believe that I am in the Father and the Father is in Me? The words I speak to you are not from Myself but the Father who lives and works in Me. **11** Believe Me, I am in the Father and the Father is in Me. If you cannot believe this, then believe because of the works.

12 "AMEN, AMEN, I say to you, whoever believes in Me will do even greater works because I am going to the Father. **13** Whatever you ask in My name I will do, so that the Father may

---

M5   The Motif of Misunderstanding appears in Jesus' spiritual statement, which is blatantly misunderstood in a materialistic way.

6   Jesus does not give answers; He gives Himself. Thomas à Kempis wrote in *Imitation of Christ,* "Without the Way there is no going, without the Truth there is no knowing, without the Life there is no living."

"No one comes to the Father except through Me." Christians must recover the boldness to act upon this statement (see Matt. 11:27; John 1:18 and 6:46; and Acts 4:12).

10   Jesus' words are reminiscent of Deuteronomy 18 and the Prophet like Moses motif.

11   Believing on the evidence of the miracles themselves puts a person in a place where genuine faith becomes possible.

12   The "greater works" will lead to redemption.

13   Jesus speaks of asking in His name, a new privilege He grants the disciples. Asking in His name means more than simply ending prayers with, "in Jesus' name." Rather, it means asking so that glory might be brought to the Father and asking in obedience to Jesus' command.

be glorified in the Son. **14** If you ask anything in My name, I will do it." 🎕

A *story from the past . . .*
Peter sat dazed. He couldn't believe his ears. For the rest of the evening I don't remember him saying a word until he spoke to the slave girl at the gate to Caiaphas's house.

We were all dazed in our own way. Jesus had warned several times already today that He was not going to be with us much longer. He kept talking about going to a place where none of us had the power to follow.

Now, finally, He told us a little about that place. He said there were many places to stay in His Father's house; that must be where He was talking about going. He assured each one of us that there would be a place just for us there, that He, always the servant, was going on ahead to make our special place ready. None of us cared what the place Jesus was talking about would be like as long as He was there.

Thomas, who was always seeking more clarity, was the one who finally asked Jesus what we all wanted to ask: "You haven't told us where it is You're going, Lord, so how could we possibly know the way?"

"I am the Way," Jesus said. "You all know Me, don't you? If you really know Me, then you know the Father; in fact, you've seen the Father if you've looked at Me. There's no other way to come to the Father except through Me."

Philip still could not grasp what He was saying. I wondered if at that point he began to doubt Jesus' sanity, as the Lord's own mother and brothers had done before (see Mark 3:21). In a nervous sort of way, the way a physician might talk to a confused, elderly patient, he said, "Then show us the Father; that will be enough."

Jesus sounded disappointed at the question. "Philip, we have been together for so long. Don't you know Me? How could you say something like that to Me? I have spoken the words of the Father. I have done the works of the Father. The Father is in Me, and I am in the Father."

179

He sounded so desperate, pleading with us to believe because of the works alone. In three years we had learned to suspect people who were always asking for signs. We had seen them come and go. And now I discovered that we, like them, were still asking Jesus to prove Himself.

THE ONE CALLED ALONGSIDE

JOHN
14:15–31

15 "If you love Me, you will keep My commands, and **16** I will ask the Father to send you another Comforter **17** who will be with you into the age. [This is] the Spirit of Truth, which the world does not have the power to recognize because it does not see Him or know Him. But you know Him because He remains with you and in you.

18 "I will not leave you as orphans; I am coming to you.

19 "In a little while the world will no longer see Me. But you see Me because I live with you and will live in you. **20** On that day you will know that I am in My Father and you in Me and I in you.

21 "Whoever has My commands and keeps them is the one who loves Me. Whoever loves Me will be loved by My Father, and I will love them and show Myself to them."

22 Judas (not Iscariot) said to Him, "Lord, what has happened that You show Yourself to us and not to the world?"

23 Jesus answered, "If anyone loves My Word, he will keep it, and My Father will love him and come to him and make a place

---

21   Our relationship with Jesus and the Father is bound up in the perfect bond of love.

23   Again, love and obedience are the only proper motives. Jesus declines to answer Judas's question but instead reiterates the call to love and obedience. The promise in verse 26 is the only answer He gives to the question.

to stay with him. **24** Whoever does not love Me does not keep the words you have heard, which are not Mine but the Father's who sent Me.

25 "I've told you all this while I'm with you, **26** but the Comforter, the Holy Spirit, which the Father will send in My name, will teach you everything and bring to your minds all the things I have told you.

27 "Peace I leave you; My peace I give to you. I do not give the way the world gives. Do not let your hearts be troubled. Don't be afraid. **28** You heard Me say I am going and I will be returning to you. If you loved Me, you would rejoice because I am going to the Father, for the Father is greater than Me.

29 "So, now I have told you before it happens so that when it happens, you may believe. **30** I will not be speaking with you much longer, for the ruler of this world is coming and he has nothing to do with Me, **31** so that the world may know how much I love the Father and that I have done all He commanded Me to do.

"Get up; let's go on from here." ✵

At the end of that memorable meal, comfort was what His disciples needed, so that is what Jesus offered them. He had spoken of His death, of their betrayal, of their not being able to follow Him where He was about to go. Now, in the midst of all the gloom, He held out a new light. "I will ask the Father to send another Comforter."

Jesus had been their first Comforter, after all, and now He was promising to send them another. As He described this new person it was as if He were describing Himself. The world will not accept this Comforter, as they had not accepted Him. The disciples would recognize Him, even as they knew Jesus, who was with them. The

---

24   This is an example of the Prophet like Moses motif. Like Moses, Jesus spoke only the words of the One who sent Him.

31   On the cross Jesus demonstrated both His love for us and His obedience to the Father; He commanded us to show the same love and obedience.

Comforter would teach them all things, just as Jesus had taught them. He would be with them forever, even as Jesus had promised to never leave them.

"I will not leave you as orphans," Jesus said. But that was what they were beginning to feel like. They had left everything to follow Him. Most of their families had turned their backs on them. And now it was becoming clear that Jesus was leaving too. What would they do? Where would they go? To hear Jesus say that another person so like Him was coming to pick up where He left off was something they all needed to hear.

He had given them a new command—to love each other— and a new example—the washing of their feet—and a new promise—they would someday have their own place in the Father's house. Now He was making a final promise: to send someone from the Father who would come alongside them. Thaddeus asked Jesus, "Why have You shown Yourself to us and not to the world?"

His question seemed to come out of nowhere, as the disciples' questions often did. But still it was a good question and one which most of us would like to hear answered. But Jesus does not take it up. Instead He reiterates the call to love and obedience. Jesus could have written His name in the stars if He had wanted. Instead He chose to show Himself to the world through the love and obedience of His followers. That would be the most convincing proof He could offer. People who ask for signs never believe them when they come, but who can deny the convicting power of a changed life? Jesus would write His name across their lives and the lives of all who would come to follow Him.

Toward the end of the discussion after their final Passover, as they reclined at the table together, Jesus repeated what He had told them at the beginning of the meal: "Do not let your hearts be troubled. Don't be afraid." In the next few hours there would be plenty to be afraid of. They would be surrounded by about two hundred soldiers in the moonlit shadows of the garden. They would be scattered, running for their lives. They would see their world come apart. They would see Him die. His words of comfort are as much a request as a consolation. Of all that they owed Him, the one thing they absolutely owed Him now was to not be afraid.

"Come now, let's go on from this place." It was the command to make their way to the garden, where the disciples hoped to finally get a chance to rest. Though they would sleep, there would be no rest for Jesus. It would be the beginning of His deep sorrow.

JOHN 15

THOSE WHO HATE ME WITHOUT A CAUSE
ARE MORE THAN THE HAIRS OF MY HEAD.

PSALM 69:4

A LONG LAST WALK

JOHN
15:1—16:4

¹ "I am the true Vine. The Father is the farmer. ² He trims off every branch in Me that does not produce fruit. Every branch that does produce fruit He trims clean so that it will produce much fruit. ³ The Word I have spoken to you has already trimmed you

---

The final verse of chapter 14 ends with the phrase, "Get up; let's go on from here." This marks the end of Jesus' discourse after the meal and the beginning of the long walk to the Garden of Gethsemane.

The discourse that follows represents the disjointedness of the walk. Jesus tends to repeat Himself from time to time as He reveals what is most on His mind. Jesus leaves six major points with His disciples and with us before He is arrested and taken away:

1. the command to remain in Him
2. the new privilege of asking in His name
3. the call to bear fruit
4. the call to love each other as we have been loved

(continued on next page)

clean. **4** Remain in Me, and I will remain in you. The branch cannot produce fruit from itself. It must remain attached to the vine; neither can you, unless you remain in Me.

5 "I am the Vine; you are the branches. Whoever remains in Me and I in them will produce much fruit. Without Me you do not have the power to do anything. **6** Whoever does not remain in Me will be cast out like a dried-up branch which is gathered up and thrown onto the fire to be burned.

7 "If you remain in Me and My words remain in you, whatever you want, ask for, and it will be done for you. **8** This will glorify My Father, that you bear much fruit and be My disciples.

9 "I have loved you the way the Father loves Me, so remain in My love. **10** You will remain in My love if you keep My commands, even as I have kept the commands of My Father and remain in His love.

11 "I have said all this to you so that you might have My joy in you and so that your joy might be full. **12** This is My command: Love one another as I have loved you. **13** No one has greater

---

5. the call to remember
6. the reason for joy

2   Jesus' allusion to Israel through the vine motif indicates that God's promise, although refused by the Jews, will be fulfilled in the new Israel (see Isa. 5:1–7, "the Song of the Vineyard"; also Jer. 2:21 and Ezek. 19:10–14).

4   Trimming and cutting off can seem to be very similar processes. In the end bearing fruit is dependent on "remaining" in Christ.

5–7   Note that these are conditional "if" statements. Only if the conditions hold true does the final phrase of verse 7 follow: "and it will be done for you." Note in the following verses how much the new privilege of asking "in His name" means to Jesus.

6   The wood from the vine is good for absolutely nothing. Sacrificial law stipulated that among wood used in sacrifice, vine wood was not to be used. Its sole purpose seems to be to live and support the bearing of fruit.

8   Praying "in Jesus' name" has to do with bringing glory to the Father, which means bearing fruit (see v. 16).

9–10   Jesus asks us to obey (and later to love) as He has obeyed the Father. He always provides the perfect pattern for our actions. If He obeyed, so should we. His life was a demonstration that it can be done.

11   It is important to note that the previous instructions are not an occasion for sullen dedication but for joy.

love than the one who lays down his life for his friends. **14** You are My friends if you do what I command.

15 "I no longer call you slaves because a slave does not know what his lord is doing. But you, I have called you friends because everything I heard from My Father I let you know about.

16 "You did not choose Me; I chose you and appointed you to go and produce much fruit, fruit that will last, so that whatever you ask the Father, in My name, He will give you.

17 "I command you: Love one another.

18 "If the world hates you, realize that it hated Me first. **19** If you were of the world, the world would have loved its own. But you are not of this world. I chose you out of the world. That is why the world hates you.

20 "Remember when I told you that a slave is not greater than his lord? If they persecute Me, they will persecute you. If they keep My word, they will keep yours too. **21** They will do all these things to you on account of My name because they do not know the One who sent Me.

22 "If I had not come and spoken to them, they would not be guilty of sin. But now, they have no excuse for the sin that wraps around them. **23** Whoever hates Me hates My Father.

24 "If I had not done among them the works which no one else ever did, they would not be guilty of sin. But they have seen and yet they still hated Me and My Father. **25** This is so the Law

---

15   Here again is the Prophet like Moses motif. Jesus has faithfully told the disciples everything He was given to say by the Father.

16   Again, bearing fruit is much on His mind, as is receiving whatever we ask for in His name.

17   This is the great summation of all that Jesus lived and taught. Note that the command to love will be followed by a discussion of hatred.

19   Jesus is telling the disciples, in effect, that it is not just that individuals out in the world hate them; every element of the world will be hostile to them.

22   Jesus earlier said that the words He spoke would condemn them on the last day (see John 12:48).

w25   John remembers Jesus quoting a psalm and referring to it as the Law. This tells us that John was aware of the authority Jesus gave to the Wisdom writings (see Pss. 35:19 and 69:4).

may be fulfilled that was written about them: 'They hated Me without a reason.'

26 "When the Comforter comes, who I will send from the Father, the Spirit of Truth which comes from the Father, He will testify about Me. **27** You also will testify, because you were with Me from the beginning.

16:1 "I have told you these things so that you will not be scandalized. **2** They will ban you from the synagogues. In fact, an hour is coming when they will believe they have served God by killing you. **3** They will do these things because they did not know the Father or Me.

4 "I have said these things to you so that you will remember that I told you when that hour comes. I didn't say anything about it in the beginning because I was with you then." ✎

A *story from the past . . .*
He was quiet during the first part of the walk that night to the Garden of Gethsemane. As we passed the temple, Jesus looked over at the large sculpted vine on one of the outer walls, and He began to speak. He pointed toward the temple and told us that He was the true vine, using the object to help make His point. He was telling a parable, like in the old days. It was good to hear one of His stories again. He said we were the branches of the vine. The only way for us branches to be fruitful would be to stay connected to the vine. It all made perfect sense to us except why, all of a sudden, would He be so concerned about our remaining in Him? What could possibly happen that would cause us to be cut off?

He gave us a new privilege: We could pray in His name. Jesus had never given us such instructions before. Now, He said, we

---

26   The picture that Jesus had just painted is one of the disciples being alone in a hostile world. They will need comfort.

27   "From the beginning" is one of John's favorite phrases.

16:1   There are two ways to stumble. Jesus is referring to the second (see Matt. 21:44; Luke 20:18; and 1 Peter 2:8).

might ask for anything in His name and the Father would give it to us.

Again and again He gave us His "new command" as if we had not been listening the first or even the fifth time He issued it. "Love each other," He kept on saying. "I have called you My friends." Then He said, almost in tears, "So love each other the way I've loved you."

Jesus could always point to Himself as the pattern for our actions. The perfect Exemplar. We were to love the way He loved, forgive the way He forgave, pray the way He prayed. After three long years at His side Jesus had never failed to perfectly live out everything He ever said. I had never known anyone with this kind of authority, the authority that came from a life perfectly lived.

He talked about the world hating Him and how we would be hated too. This was nothing new to our experience. Many of our families hated us for following Him. Every day for the past year we had sensed the hatred from some in the crowd, particularly the priests and Pharisees. Only now He explained why they hated us so. It was, He said, because we did not belong to the world but to Him, because He had chosen us out of all the world. Jesus said they had heard His words and seen the works of God in His life and still they hated Him. How could that be?

He said the Writings had promised He would be hated without a reason. But they are guilty all the same, He told us. If they had not seen, all would be as it had been before. But now they had heard and seen—but still refused His Word; now that Word would condemn them on the last day. "Someday they will think that if they kill you, they will be doing God a favor," He said as we crossed the stream in the moonlight just before the garden gate. "Remember that I told you all this before it happened. And wait for the Comforter."

PROVING THE WORLD WAS WRONG

JOHN
16:5–18

5 "Now I am returning to the One who sent Me, yet none of you asks, 'Where are You going?' **6** Your hearts are full of sorrow because of the things I've said. **7** But, I tell you the truth, it is better for you that I go away because if I do not go the Comforter will

---

5 Note "to the One who sent Me," Jesus' most frequent circumlocution for God. Jesus is the One who was "sent."

7 Jesus' going away is a necessity before the Comforter can come. *Paraklatos,* the Greek word translated "Comforter," is composed of two parts: *para,* meaning "beside," and *kaleo,* meaning "to be called." The *paraklatos* is the one who is called alongside to give comfort. Others suggest that this word might be translated "counselor." Given the context of verse 6, "your hearts

(continued on next page)

not come to you. If I go, I will send Him to you. **8** When He comes He will show that the world was wrong about sin and righteousness and judgment:

9 "About sin—because they do not believe in Me,

10 "About righteousness—because I go to the Father, where you will no longer see Me,

11 "About judgment—because the ruler of this world has already been judged.

12 "There are so many things I have yet to tell you. But you could not bear to hear them now. **13** When the Spirit of Truth comes, He will guide you into every truth. He will not speak from Himself but only the things He hears. And He will disclose to you what is to come. **14** He will glorify Me by taking from what is mine and disclosing it to you.

15 "Everything which the Father has is Mine. That is why I said, 'He will take from what is Mine and disclose it to you.'

---

are full of sorrow," along with the mention of *orphanos* (comfortless), the "Comforter" translation seems best.

Jesus told the disciples the Spirit would:

1. Guide you to all truth.
2. Speak only what He hears, as Jesus did (see Deut. 18).
3. Tell you what is to come.
4. Bring glory to Jesus by taking from the things that belong to Jesus and the Father and showing them to us.

8   When the Spirit comes, He will prove the world is wrong about three things:

1. Sin—the world says it is an offense against the status quo. The Spirit defines it as not believing in Jesus.
2. Righteousness—Jesus' return to the Father will be the final demonstration that He was truly righteous.
3. Judgment—Jesus will define judgment on the cross. That is where judgment of the world takes place.

13   Even as Jesus repeatedly stated that He only spoke the things He heard from the Father, so now the Spirit will only speak what He hears (see Deut. 18). Meditate on what it means to only speak what you have heard from the Father.

16 "A little while longer and you will not see Me. Then after a little while, you will see Me."

17 Some of the disciples said to each other, "What is this He is saying to us, 'In a little while you will not see Me and then in a little while you will see Me,' and 'Because I go to the Father.' **18** What is 'a little time'"? they said. "We do not understand what He is saying." ✼

It must have been hard for the disciples to hear Jesus say that it was better for them that He go away so that the Spirit could come. Jesus, they knew. This "Comforter," they did not think they knew, even though Jesus told them, in fact, they did.

As they approach Gethsemane, Jesus tells the disciples of the many things the coming of the Spirit will do. After the coming of Jesus, the world would never be the same. Jesus' coming had changed all the rules, shattered all the definitions. It would be the Spirit's mission to convince the world that it was wrong about the three central concepts of "religion": the definitions of sin, righteousness, and judgment.

Most religions, especially Judaism, are based on a keen sensitivity to what sin is. The rabbis rightly hated sin and used the Law to build a fence around the people to protect them from it. It was their passionate goal in life to live sinlessly. By Jesus' day it had become a task so filled with technicalities that only the full-time professionals could hope to come close to this kind of perfection.

The Comforter would define sin in a completely unheard-of way. Sin was not a matter of perfectionism, of keeping all the rules, of maintaining the status quo. Sin was a matter of not believing in Jesus, whose death made perfect provision for the forgiveness of the world's sin. The world said sin is something you do. The Spirit would show them that sin is something you are, something that only believing in Christ can undo.

ᴹ**17**   This verse is an example of the Motif of Misunderstanding.

If sin were to be redefined, then its opposite, righteousness, had to be reconsidered as well. It was widely taught, as it still is today, that righteousness was also a matter of keeping the rules. But Jesus had been an abominable rule-keeper. He spat on the Sabbath. He commanded people to carry burdens on the Sabbath. He and His disciples gathered grain on the Sabbath. Jesus displayed little concern, if not outright contempt at times, for their rules. Therefore, Jesus was judged "unrighteous" by the Jews. In their eyes He would never be eligible to enter heaven, the true goal of all the righteous.

The Spirit, Jesus told them, would prove that the world was wrong about righteousness when it revealed to them the fact that Jesus had indeed returned to His Father. The Manna that had descended would also ascend to heaven and the "One who sent Him." The world was wrong, and Jesus' return to the Father would prove it.

New concepts of sin and righteousness inevitably lead us to a new definition of judgment. Judgment is the consequence of whatever you define sin and righteousness to be.

The world defined judgment as a consequence, as a simple matter of cause and effect. If you were a sinner you would be judged. If you were righteous, you would escape judgment. But with the rolling away of the stone from Jesus' tomb, that definition was also shattered.

The world will not be judged in some future event, Jesus said. The prince of this world, the devil, now stands condemned. Judgment would happen on the cross of Jesus, the cross that was the judgment of the world. There the world would be found guilty, and the full penalty for its sin would be inflicted on the sinless, solitary Son of God. The price for the sins of the whole world would be paid there. In the blood of His own Son, God would mark the debt canceled.

The implications for us of these new definitions of sin, righteousness, and judgment are often unrealized. Sin, indeed the unpardonable sin, is failure to believe in Jesus. Righteousness belongs only to Him who is now with the Father. Judgment has already taken place, and we were found guilty. But the One who was our Judge is also our Savior. We escaped judgment precisely because

He did not. Now our righteousness is to be found only through Him.

Again, regretfully, all the disciples seem to hear is Jesus' last few words, "I am going away for a little time." It is their almost continual condition of misunderstanding that the Spirit will cure.

"I HAVE CONQUERED THE WORLD"

JOHN
16:19–33

19 Jesus knew what they wanted to ask Him and so He said to them, "You're asking each other about what I said, 'In a little while you will not see Me and then in a little while you will see Me again'?

20 "AMEN, AMEN, I say to you, you will weep and mourn, but the world will rejoice. You will grieve, but your grief will become joy. **21** When a woman is giving birth, she suffers because her hour has come. But when she gives birth, she forgets her suffering because of the joy that someone has been born into the world. **22** Now is your time of grief, but I will see you again and your hearts will rejoice, and this joy no one will ever take away from you. **23** On that day you will not ask Me anything. AMEN, AMEN, I say to you, whatever you ask the Father in My name He will give you. **24** Until now you have not asked in My name. Ask, and you will receive, so that your joy may be full.

25 "I have spoken to you in metaphors. The hour is coming when I will quit speaking metaphorically but plainly concerning the Father. **26** On that day you will ask in My name, I am not saying

---

21   Note the image of the woman in childbirth, and then read Isaiah 13:8; 21:3; 26:17; and 42:14; and Micah 4:9ff. This is prophetic imagery.

25   Literally, Jesus is saying, "I have been speaking in parables" (see Ps. 78:2). His parables have involved the vine and branches, and the woman in travail.

that I will ask the Father for you, **27** for the Father Himself loves you because you have loved Me and believed that I came from God.

28 "I came from the Father and have come into the world. Now I am leaving the world and returning to the Father."

29 The disciples said to Him, "See, now You are speaking plainly and not in metaphors. **30** Now we know that You know all things and do not need to ask anyone questions. Because of this we believe that You have come from God."

31 Jesus answered them, "Do you really believe? **32** Look, the hour is coming and has now come when you will be scattered and leave Me alone. But I am not alone, because the Father is with Me. **33** I have told you these things so that you might have peace, in Me. In the world you will have suffering, but have courage; I have conquered the world." ✀

Y ou will weep, you will mourn, you will grieve like a woman having a baby," Jesus tells them as He lifts the latch of the garden gate. "You will be scattered like sheep and will leave Me to fend for Myself, all alone. All the while the world will rejoice." Minutes before He had spoken of zealots who would seek to kill them for God's sake. "The Light," He said, "is only with you for a little while longer."

They have only a few hours left to be together. It has been a long, dark evening. It will get darker still. Jesus has painted a hostile picture of the world for His disciples as indeed it will be. All but one of them will die a martyr's death. And though this may seem to be reality on the surface, it is not the true, deep spiritual reality that Jesus had come to reveal to them. Before He turns to pray to the Father for Himself, for them, and for us, He speaks a final word of comfort, the greatest words of comfort He ever spoke: "I have told you these things so that you might have peace, in Me. In the

---

28 This seems to finally be an answer to the question that was originally asked in verse 5, "Where are You going?" Before, the disciples were confused. Now they seem to understand.

31 Perhaps Jesus speaks with a tone of irony: "Do you really believe?"

world you will have suffering, but have courage; I have conquered the world."

Nothing could have seemed more unlikely to them at the moment. Jesus is a hunted man, in hiding from those in power. By all accounts the world is about to conquer Him. But that is not the truth, and Jesus wants His disciples to know.

JOHN 17

I HAVE BEEN ESTABLISHED
FROM EVERLASTING,
FROM THE BEGINNING, BEFORE THERE
WAS EVER AN EARTH.

PROVERBS 8:23

THE TIME
HAS COME

JOHN
17:1–26

1 After He said these things Jesus lifted His eyes to heaven and said, "Father, the hour has come. Glorify Your Son so that Your Son may glorify You. **2** You gave Me authority over all flesh so that I could give life eternal to all You have given Me.

3 "This is eternal life, that they might learn to know You, the only true God and the One You sent, Jesus Christ.

4 "I have glorified You on earth. I have finished the work You gave Me to do. **5** Now glorify Me, along with Yourself, Father, with the glory I possessed with You before the world was.

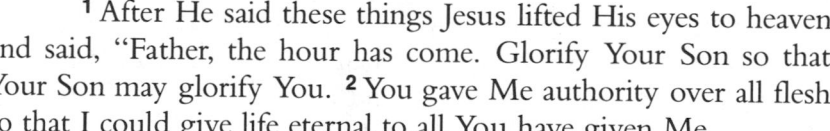

3 Jesus' definition of eternal life: knowing God, knowing Jesus.

6 "I revealed Your name to the ones You gave Me out of the world. They were Yours. You gave them to Me. They kept Your Word. **7** Now they know that all You gave Me indeed came from You. **8** I gave them the words You gave Me. They accepted them. They know truly that I came from You. They believe You sent Me.

9 "I am asking for their sakes, not the world, but for these ones You have given Me, because they are Yours, **10** and all that is Mine is Yours, and all that is Yours is Mine. I have been glorified in them.

11 "I am leaving the world, but they are still in the world. I'm coming to You, Holy Father. So keep them in Your name, in the name You gave Me, so that they may be one as We are.

12 "When I was with them I kept them in Your name, the name You gave Me. I kept watch over them, and none of them has died except the son of death, so that the Scripture might be fulfilled.

13 "Now, I am coming to You. I have said these things while I was in the world so that they might have My joy filling themselves. **14** I have given them Your Word, and the world has hated them for it. They are not of the world just as I am not of the world.

15 "I'm not asking You to take them out of the world, but please keep them from the evil. **16** They are not of the world, just as I am not of the world.

17 "Set them apart in the truth. Your Word is the truth.

18 "As you sent Me into the world, now I'm sending them into the world. **19** For their sakes I set Myself apart that they may also be truly set apart.

20 "It is not only for these that I ask, but also for the ones who will believe in Me because of their word, **21** that all of us may be one, as You, Father, are in Me and I am in You, let them be in Us. This way the world will believe that You sent Me. **22** The glory

---

10b   Jesus says that glory had come to Him through His disciples. Can the same be said of you and me?

12   There is a play on words here: "None of them has died except the son of death."

20   Note how often Jesus mentions future believers. We are much on His mind.

You gave Me, I give to them so that they may be one, as We are one. **23** I in them, You in Me, that they may be perfectly one, that the world may know that You sent Me and loved them as You loved Me.

24 "Father, I want these ones You have given Me to be with Me where I am so that they can see My glory, which You gave Me before the foundation of the world, because You loved Me.

25 "Righteous Father, the world did not recognize You, but I know You, and these ones know that You sent Me. **26** I let them know Your name and will make it known so that the love You have for Me will be in them as I am in them." ✸

I can remember when I was eight years old someone showing me this passage in John and pointing out the place where Jesus prayed for all those who would become His followers. I can remember vividly the thrill of realizing that Jesus Christ had thought to pray for me. It was not long after that time that I gave my life to become one of His disciples. It was that insight that made me begin to feel as if I could really come to know Him. For if you really want to know someone's heart, listen to them pray. Prayer is the truest way to reveal yourself, not only to God, but to those around you. Perhaps that's why so many of us are reluctant to lead prayer in public. We do not want to be discovered.

Jesus prays to the Father before He enters the "place of crushing," the Garden of Gethsemane. This prayer is the prelude to the prayer that will cause Him to sweat drops of blood.

The thought of glory is much on His mind. He prays for the glorification of the Father through Him, and He prays for His own glorification. He speaks of having given to His disciples the glory the Father had given to Him. Incredibly, He even speaks of the disciples' having brought Him glory.

---

23 Jesus asks that we may be brought together in perfect unity. In the same breath He mentions love, which is the perfect bond (Col. 3:14). God lavishes His love on us through Christ. Before Jesus you cannot deny the fact that God loves you.

The prospect that we might bring glory to Jesus by being His disciples is almost more than the mind can contain. As the darkness closes in around Him, Jesus clings to this hope of glory as a way to keep His mind clear or perhaps as a way to keep His mind at all. His recollection of the preincarnate glory He shared with the Father, "before there was ever an earth," was, for Him, a light to shine against the dark forces that were gathering all around Him.

"Give glory to your Son that your Son might give glory to You," Jesus prays. Within the context of God's love the distinction between giving and receiving disappears. It becomes meaningless. We have all experienced this in the giving of gifts, when the act of offering the gift becomes, in itself, a way of receiving; when the act of giving becomes a gift. Jesus prays for glory, not for Himself but so that He might give it to the Father as a gift.

It seems that as His earthly ministry comes to a close all the new definitions Jesus has brought about are coming to the surface. In the middle of His prayer Jesus gives us the new definition of eternal life. Before, we thought of eternal life in terms of quantity: life that never ends. Jesus opens the door to an entirely different understanding when He defines eternal life simply as knowing God. This new definition embraces the present moment for all those who know God. Eternal life has already begun. It begins the moment we come to know God through Jesus Christ.

Jesus' concern for the safety of His disciples is touching; you can hear the compassion in His voice as He prays for them and for us. At a time when anyone else would be consumed with self-centered thoughts, Jesus asks that the protection He afforded them, by way of the name of the Father, be extended to them when He leaves. He watched over them, like the Good Shepherd; now as they go out into a wolf-filled world, Jesus asks the Father to keep watch. He has been able to protect all of them but one, Judas, the son of death, who even now is at the high priest's gathering together the posse to take Jesus away to be crucified.

One final thought keeps racing through His mind: oneness. Jesus repeats more than once the idea that He and the Father are one. He seems almost to be working through some sort of holy equation: "You are in Me, Father, and I am in You. Let them become one in Us. I in them and You in Me." The perfect bond of this oneness is love.

Jesus speaks the remarkable notion that the Father has loved them with the same love He extended to His Son. God lavishes His love on us through Christ. You cannot look at Jesus and deny the fact that God is love. It is Jesus who makes it possible for God to love us the way He loves His Son by removing the barrier of our sin.

Again and again in John's Gospel it has been said, "His time had not yet come." Now that time *has* come. Jesus knows it, so He goes to prayer. He has seemed so cut off and lonely through most of the narrative, except when it comes to the Father. He never seems to lose sight of the "One who sent Me." Soon the One who sent Him will send Him to a place where even He cannot, because of His holiness, follow. And Jesus will be completely alone. But, for now, the thoughts that fill His prayers are of glory, oneness, and joy.

A FULL-MOON SEARCH

JOHN
18:1–12

¹ After He said these things Jesus departed with His disciples across the Kidron ravine. He and His disciples entered the garden which was there. ² Judas, the one who was betraying Him, also knew the place because Jesus often met with His disciples there.

³ Judas came with a cohort of soldiers and some of the chief

---

3 The word John uses to designate the detachment of soldiers, *speria,* indicates a force of two hundred to six hundred men. These are Roman soldiers, stationed in the Tower of Antonia. It is Passover, which means there was a full moon, and yet they carried torches. This indicates they were expecting a search.

priests and Pharisees' attendants. They carried torches, lamps, and weapons.

4 Jesus knew everything that was coming upon Him. He went out to them and said, "Who are you looking for?"

5 They answered Him, "Jesus, the Nazarene."

"I am," He said to them. (Judas, the betrayer, was standing there with them.)

6 When He said, "I am," they retreated and fell to the ground.

7 He asked them again, "Who are you looking for?"

"Jesus, the Nazarene," they said.

8 Jesus told them, "I told you, I am. If I am the one you are looking for, then let these men go."

9 (This was so His word would be fulfilled, "I have lost none of the ones You have given Me.")

10 Simon Peter, who had a sword, drew it and struck the high priest's servant, cutting off his right ear. His name was Malchus.

11 Jesus said to Peter, "Put the sword back into its sheath. Shouldn't I drink the cup the Father has given Me?"

---

6 This verse contains the actions of both the Roman soldiers and the Jews who had come to arrest Jesus. When the Jews heard Jesus pronounce the divine name, "I am," they fell down in fear. If ever the name was spoken by someone who was unclean, that person would be destroyed. The Jews feared they would be caught in the fallout of Jesus' destruction.

The soldiers "retreated." This describes a military maneuver in response to what the soldiers thought was an ambush. They had expected a search, but Jesus walked right up to them. Now they fear the trap is about to be sprung.

9 This is one of the first examples of one of Jesus' predictions being fulfilled (see John 6:39).

ᴰ**10** It was against the law to carry any weapon on the Passover. Earlier in the garden, Jesus had been talking to the disciples about selling their coats and buying swords (Luke 22:36). At the arrest they respond by saying, "Should we strike with our swords?" (Luke 22:49).

We further see John's detailed knowledge of Jerusalem. He knows the name of the high priest's servant. Luke, the doctor, tells us that it was the "little ear," or earlobe, that Peter hacked off. This would indicate a horizontal swipe of the sword and perhaps an attempt to cut the throat or even sever the head. Malchus turns his head at the last moment and only loses an earlobe.

12 The band of soldiers, the commander of the cohort, and the servants of the Jews arrested Jesus and tied Him up. ✵

A *story from the past . . .*
The Cedar Valley was a place we often rested, trying to escape the noise of the feast crowds. Jesus liked being away from the busyness of town. We could always find branches on the ground to use for fire.

It was already late as we made our way through the garden gate. He seemed to have said all He had to say. We walked slowly behind Him, confused and afraid.

The moon was full, so there was no problem seeing where we were going. It cast our shadows back behind us. No one had much to say. Jesus had already said so much. We tried to think about all He had said as we settled down to sleep for the night. Jesus went off, alone, to pray.

I first heard the sound of their feet coming through the ground as my ear was pressed against it in sleep. There were hundreds of them, their torches casting an angry glow. Jesus had said earlier that a time was coming when we would need to sell our coats to buy swords, but none of us thought it would be so soon.

Then all at once, I saw Judas at the head of the throng. "It's all right," I said to the others. "Judas is with them."

But everything was not right.

They halted just inside the gate. The soldiers were nervous. They kept straining their eyes, trying to see beyond the shadows. They kept their hands on their weapons. They were expecting a fight.

Jesus broke away from us and walked over to the commanding officer, who was standing with Judas and some of the Jews. "Who are you looking for?" He calmly asked.

The captain of the guard answered in a military tone, "Jesus the Nazarene."

---

12   Only John informs us that Jesus was first taken to Annas's house to be held while the Sanhedrin could be called for an illegal nighttime meeting. Annas was perhaps the most powerful man in Jerusalem at the time. The fact that Jesus was held in his home indicates his active involvement in the plot.

207

"I am," Jesus said.

The priests and Pharisees fell to the ground at hearing the sound of the unspeakable name. The soldiers, however, who were Romans, thought it was the signal for an ambush. They believed they had walked right into a trap. They drew back in military fashion, ready to fight.

It was a sight I will never forget. The priests hugging the ground, the sound of swords coming out of their sheaths, soldiers forming lines in preparation for an attack that would never come. And in the middle of them all, Jesus stood calmly, asking once again, "Who did you say you were looking for?"

Slowly they all rose from the ground, regaining their composure. "Jesus the Nazarene," they muttered, brushing the sand from their leather breeches.

"I told you, I am," He said. "You have Me. Now let these men go." He motioned back to us as we stood in the fading shadows. A few of the soldiers had come around behind us in a flanking maneuver. Along with them were a few servants of the high priest, excited at taking part in such an operation. Just as one of them, Malchus, a man I knew from my father's fishmarket, got close to where we were standing, Simon reached inside the folds of his robe and brandished a short sword. With both hands he made a horizontal swipe at the neck of the high priest's servant, hoping, I suppose, to cut off his head. At the last moment Malchus turned his head and fell back. It looked as if the tip of Peter's sword caught his earlobe. I thought I remembered seeing blood. But Jesus rushed over and helped the frightened man up. A few minutes later when I saw Malchus again, his ear seemed fine.

Jesus looked at Simon and told him sternly to put his sword back into its sheath. The high priests might have arrested Peter for simply carrying a weapon on a feast day, but Jesus was firm when He asked that we be let go. Perhaps the Jews knew arresting us would only make for another fight.

Seeing them tie Jesus' hands behind His back made us all feel as if we were somehow being bound up too. As they pushed Him on His way, Jesus gave us a look that told us to run, but Peter and I followed at a safe distance to see what would happen next.

THE TRIALS

JOHN
18:13–40

13 First they led Him to Annas because he was the father-in-law of Caiaphas, who was high priest that year. **14** It was Caiaphas who counseled the Jews that it was better for one man to die for the people.

15 Simon Peter and another disciple followed Jesus. The high priest knew the other disciple, so he was allowed into the court of the high priest with Jesus. **16** Peter had to stand outside the door. The other disciple, the one who was known to the high priest, went and spoke to the doorkeeper and brought Peter in. **17** The girl who was doorkeeper said to Peter, "You aren't another of this man's disciples, are you?"

He said, "I am not."

18 The slaves and servants were warming themselves around a fire they had made because it was cold. Peter stood there with them, warming himself.

19 The high priest questioned Jesus about His disciples and His teaching.

20 "I have spoken in public to the world," Jesus said. "I always taught in the synagogue and the temple where all the Jews congregate. I said nothing in secret. **21** So why are you questioning Me? Ask the ones who heard what I said. Look, they know what I said."

22 But when He said this one of the servants standing nearby

---

20   Jesus reminds Annas of a point of law that dates back to the code of Maimonides: Someone cannot be convicted on the basis of his or her own testimony.

struck Jesus with a rod. He said, "Is that any way to answer the high priest?"

23 Jesus answered, "If I spoke badly, tell Me what was bad, but if it was good, why did you beat Me?"

24 Then they sent Him from Annas to Caiaphas. He was tied up.

25 Simon Peter was still standing and warming himself. They said to him, "You are not another of His disciples, are you?"

He answered, "I am not."

26 One of the slaves of the high priest, a relative of the one whose ear Peter had cut off, said, "Didn't I see you in the garden with Him?"

27 Again Peter denied it. Immediately a rooster crowed.

28 Then they led Jesus from Caiaphas to the Praetorium. It was still early, and they would not go in, afraid they might be

---

ᴰ26 Here John demonstrates more local knowledge by telling us he knows this servant is a relative of Malchus.

Perhaps this is a good place to share three interesting details from the life of Pilate:

When Pilate ordered the Roman standards installed in the temple (the standards were actually small idols the soldiers offered incense to) the Jews protested. A group followed him all the way to Caesarea, hounding him to have the standards removed. Pilate met the group in the amphitheater, telling them to leave or be executed. When the Jews bared their necks to the soldiers, Pilate relented.

In order to build an aqueduct for Jerusalem, Pilate stole money from the treasury at the temple. Because of this, the people rioted, but he had the crowd infiltrated with soldiers in plain clothes. At his order they struck out at the crowd, and hundreds were killed.

Because of mass executions in Samaria, carried out by Pilate, he was ordered back to Rome to be judged by Tiberias, who died while Pilate was on the way. At that point Pilate vanished; many scholars believe he committed suicide along the way.

28 The Jews had to have a judgment from Pilate early in the morning since this would be the only time he could be reached. Business was taken care of early in the day so that the remainder of the day could be spent in a full schedule of Roman leisure activities.

The Jews want to avoid uncleanness so that they can eat the Friday night Passover. These are Judean Jews. Jesus' disciples followed the tradition of the Diaspora Jews, who ate Passover on Thursday night.

211

rendered ritually unclean. They wanted to be able to eat Passover. **29** So Pilate came outside to them. He said, "What charge are you bringing against this man?"

30 They answered, "If He were not doing evil, we would not have handed Him over to you."

31 Pilate said, "Take Him away and judge Him according to your law."

The Jews said, "It is unlawful for us to kill anyone."

32 (This was so the word of Jesus would be fulfilled that indicated the kind of death He was about to die.)

33 Pilate went back into the Praetorium and summoned Jesus. "You are the king of the Jews?" he said to Him.

34 Jesus answered, "Do you say this from yourself, or did someone else tell you about Me?"

35 "I am not a Jew, am I? Your own people and the high priest handed You over to me. What did You do?"

36 Jesus answered, "My kingdom is not of this world. If it was My kingdom, My servants would have fought to keep Me from being handed over to the Jews. But now My kingdom is not from here."

37 "So you are a king," Pilate answered.

Jesus said, "You say that I am a king. I was born for this and have come into the world to testify to the truth. Everyone who is of the truth hears My voice."

38 "What is truth?" Pilate said to Him. With that he went back out to the Jews and said to them, "I find no cause for accusation against Him. **39** But there is a custom that I may release to you one prisoner during Passover. Do you want me to release the king of the Jews?"

40 They howled, "Not Him! Barabbas!" (Barabbas was an insurrectionist.) ✵

---

29   The tone of Pilate's voice in this verse is no doubt formal: "Let's hurry up and get this over with!" His mind is on the exercise and baths that await him.

32   This is another example of Jesus' words being fulfilled. He would be "lifted up," or crucified, on a high Roman cross.

40   Barabbas is genuinely guilty of the charge that Jesus will be falsely convicted of.

Wwith the arrest of Jesus a series of mock trials began. If ever two societies were meticulous about legal proceedings it was Israel and Rome. However, in every step of the proceedings against Jesus the most basic tenets of the law were broken. Throughout the trial Jesus is constantly reminding them about proper legal procedure.

There were basically two trials: one Jewish, one Roman. Each trial had three parts.

The Jewish Proceedings

Part one: Immediately after being arrested Jesus was bound and taken to the home of Annas, who was in all likelihood the key conspirator behind the plot to have Jesus killed. The marketplace in the temple, which Jesus had twice destroyed, was called the Bazaar of Annas. It belonged to him. Caiaphas had married Annas's daughter. Annas had been high priest some fifteen years earlier but had been removed from office by the Romans. Jesus was held here while the members of the Sanhedrin, the Jewish ruling council, could be called together.

In the courtyard of the high priest's house, huddled by the fire, Peter denied Jesus. John, who has local knowledge, knew the girl at the door. He was able to get Peter by the guards and into the yard. The girl knew that John was a follower of Jesus, because when she saw Peter she asked if he was "another" of Jesus' disciples. Mark tells us Peter's Galilean accent betrayed him as a follower of Jesus. So John is there as a known disciple. Peter is too afraid of being arrested.

Luke gives us the chilling detail that upon denying Jesus for the third time Peter's eyes met Jesus' across the courtyard. It was this painful moment that caused Peter to run away, weeping bitterly (Luke 22:61).

Meanwhile, at the home of Annas, the preliminary interrogation began. Jesus was questioned about His disciples and His teachings. Jesus reminded Annas of the law, that a man could not be convicted by his own testimony. The facts had to be established by two or more witnesses. At the formal hearing the high priest responded by calling several false witnesses whose testimonies contradicted each other.

One of the servants struck Jesus with a staff for making this point. This also was in violation of the law.

Part two: Next Jesus was taken to the home of Caiaphas. This was the primary Jewish trial. John omits the details of this segment of the proceedings. Here, before the council, which had illegally come together during the night, the formal charge of blasphemy was formulated, based on Jesus' own confession that He was the Son of God. It was here that they spat at Jesus and blindfolded Him, striking Him in the face and demanding that He tell who struck Him.

Part three: At daylight, a mock trial before the Sanhedrin was held to ratify the midnight decision (see Mark 15:1 and Luke 22:66). John also omits this detail, knowing it was contained in the Synoptics. At this trial the charge of sedition against Rome was concocted so that formal charges might be brought against Jesus before Pilate.

The Roman Trials

Part one: Because of his full schedule of Roman leisure, Pilate, like any Roman official, would take care of business early in the morning before heading off to the spas. Knowing this, the Jews brought Jesus to the Praetorium early in the morning, between 6:00 and 7:00.

When Pilate asked for the charge, the Jews responded only by saying if Jesus were not guilty, they would not have brought Him. This was not a charge, so Pilate took Jesus, who refused to answer questions in public by now, into the judgment hall for a private interrogation.

During their talk Jesus began to speak about the truth. Pilate, responding more from impatience than sincerity, asked, "What is truth?" and immediately turned and walked out the door. He was not able to find reason to have Jesus bound over for the crime. During the questioning Pilate discovered that Jesus was from Galilee, where his old enemy, Herod, served as tetrarch. As a token of reconciliation and to get Jesus out of his hair, Pilate sent Jesus to Herod.

Part two: Luke tells us that Herod was pleased to see Jesus. This is the same Herod who murdered John the Baptist. He was curious to see Jesus perform a trick.

Jesus refused to answer Herod's questions. It was at the trial before Herod that the soldiers mocked Jesus, dressing Him in an elegant robe. Seeing that he was getting nowhere, Herod sent Jesus back to Pilate. Luke tells us that from that day on, Herod and Pilate became friends.

Part three: At last Jesus was dragged back to Pilate. To appease them, he had Jesus flogged. It was here that the soldiers fashioned a crown of thorns and pressed it down around His head—all this without a single accusation being proven against Him. In the meantime, Pilate received word from his wife that she had had disturbing dreams about Jesus, who she called an "innocent man."

In a flagrant violation of Roman law, Pilate offered to hand Jesus over to the mob to be crucified, saying he could find no basis for a charge against Him. When he heard the crowd say that Jesus had made the claim of being the Son of God, Pilate took Him back into the palace. He questioned Jesus, asking Him if He realized the severity of the situation.

Jesus seemed to give Pilate the benefit of the doubt by telling him that the Jews who handed Him over to Pilate were guilty of a greater sin than Pilate's in condemning Jesus.

Because of this gracious response from Jesus, Pilate tried to have Jesus set free, but he finally gave in to the threats of the crowd and made a formal ruling against Him. Jesus would be executed after the Roman fashion so His word concerning the kind of death He would die would be fulfilled. He would be "lifted up" to die on a high Roman cross.

A FRIEND OF SEJANUS, NO FRIEND OF CAESAR

JOHN
19:1–16

1 So Pilate had Jesus taken and flogged. **2** The soldiers wove a wreath of thorns and put it on His head. They threw a purple robe around Him. **3** They came up to Him and said, "Hail, the king of the Jews." And they struck Him with their fists.

---

1 Note this was not a Jewish flogging as mentioned by Paul in 2 Corinthians 11. That would have involved thirty-nine stripes with a rod. It was the Romans who flogged Jesus, and the only stipulation about flogging in Roman law was that a man would be flogged until the flesh hung from his back. Roman flogging was administered not by rods but by the cruel flagrum, a whip of many strands with plaited bits of bone and glass in the ends. Men were sometimes disemboweled by a Roman flogging. The movies and sermons that portray this as the "forty save one" miss the mark considerably.

3 Literally, this verse is translated "kept giving Him blows with their hands."

4 Pilate came out again and told them, "Look, I am bringing Him back out to you so you will know that I have found no fault with Him."

5 Then Jesus came outside, wearing the thorny wreath and the purple robe.

He said to them, "Behold, the man!"

6 When the chief priests and the attendants saw Him standing they howled, "Crucify, crucify!"

"Take Him yourselves and crucify Him," Pilate said to them. "I find no fault in Him."

7 The Jews answered, "We have a law, and according to that law He ought to die because He made Himself out to be the Son of God."

8 When Pilate heard this, he was even more afraid. **9** He went back into the Praetorium and said to Jesus, "Where are You from?"

Jesus did not give him an answer.

10 "So, You will not speak to me?" Pilate said. "Don't You know that I have the authority to free You, and I have the authority to crucify You?"

11 Jesus answered him, "You have absolutely no authority against Me except what has been given you from above. So those who handed Me over to you have committed a greater sin."

12 From then on Pilate began to try to free Him. But the Jews shouted, "If you free this man, you are not a friend of Caesar. Anyone who makes himself a king is speaking against Caesar."

13 When Pilate heard these words, he led Jesus out. He sat on a judicial bench in a place called the Pavement (in Hebrew, *Gabbatha*).

14 It was the day for preparation of the Passover, about the sixth hour. He said to the Jews, "Behold your king!"

---

7   The Jews are referring here to Leviticus 24:14–16.

13   The "stone pavement" was traditionally a place where judgment was pronounced. When Julius Caesar was on campaign, he carried a portable mosaic pavement with him for this purpose. It is at the moment when Pilate arrives at the pavement that Pilate's wife sends word to him to have nothing to do with this "innocent man."

14   The Day of Preparation was the day when the Jerusalemite Jews were "preparing" their lambs for sacrifice. Jesus, the Lamb of God, is sacrificed at precisely the same time as the other lambs. One wonders if the sound of their bleating was heard along with His own shouts from the cross.

15 They shouted, "Away, away! Crucify Him!"

"Shall I crucify your king?" Pilate said to them.

The high priest answered, "The only king we have is Caesar."

16 Then he handed Him over to be crucified. ✄

The morning had not gone well for either of them. All Pilate wanted was to be rid of the noisy, troublemaking Jews. Jesus, too, seemed to want it all to be over.

They had been dragging Him from place to place since His arrest in the garden. He had been struck with rods, He had been slapped in the face, blindfolded, and spat upon. They had dressed Him up in robes and horse blankets. They had woven a crown of thorns and pressed it down on His head. It was supposed to be a joke, but no one laughed when they saw Him with the blood dripping down His cheeks.

Pilate was shouting to the Jews that after all his investigation he had found no reason for Jesus to be condemned. As he leaned over the railing and addressed the crowd, he noticed a hush coming over them. He looked back in time to see Jesus staggering out of the palace. He was a bloody mess. His hair was matted with blood. Blood had soaked through the robe the soldiers had wrapped around His shoulders. Even His feet were dripping with blood so that He left bright red footprints as He stumbled onto the porch.

"Here is the man!" Pilate said to them in as unassuming a voice as he could muster. Here is the man who is only a man after all. He bleeds like a man, he cries out in pain like a man, and if this charade is not stopped soon, he will die like a man.

The crowd was insistent. They howled like a pack of wolves. The blood madness was coming over them. Nothing less than this man's death would appease them.

"Take Him yourselves and crucify Him," Pilate said, shrugging his shoulders. His mind raced at the possibilities. On one hand they should never be allowed to take the life of a prisoner, even one who

---

ᴰ**15**   Note that John gives us the detail that it was not the rabble who shouted "The only king we have is Caesar," but the very priests. Some have called this the formal abdication of the Messianic hope.

was guilty of much less than this innocent man. On the other hand, if they did the work themselves, he might be able later to convict some of them for murder. His mind was weighing all the possibilities. He was imagining the joy of condemning someone like Caiaphas, of seeing him hanging from a high cross, overlooking his own temple. A single sentence from the crowd woke him from his musings. It was like someone splashed cold water on his face.

"He said He was the Son of God," someone yelled.

Pilate turned without a word and went back into the palace. Jesus followed dutifully behind him.

"Where did You come from?" he asked as he looked intently into Jesus' bloody face. He asked as if he were expecting to hear the answer "heaven."

By now this all seemed so useless to Jesus, who knew exactly what was before Him. His eyes slowly closed as if He were about to faint.

"What is the matter with You!" Pilate screamed two inches from his face. "I could free You; I have the power. Or I could let the mob have their way and have You nailed to a cross." He threatened Jesus like a schoolyard bully.

Jesus, in pain and exhaustion, whispered, "You have no power, only what has been given to you from heaven. The ones outside are more guilty than you."

It was remarkable to Pilate that Jesus spoke with no bitterness. He felt as if Jesus would have forgiven him for what he had done to Him so far—if Pilate had had it in himself to ask for forgiveness. *That's it,* he thought to himself. *This man is going to go free.*

Pilate rose to his feet, clapping his hands to summon the guard. *They can escort Jesus out of the city where He will be safe.* As he strode across the marble floor he heard a single voice rising above the noise of the crowd. Though it was a scream outside, by the time it reached his ears inside the thick walls of the Praetorium it sounded like a whisper.

"If you let Him go you are no friend of Caesar."

He stopped, leaning against a cool stone column. "Friend of Caesar" was a formal title he had been granted by the emperor himself. He had risen so far. Who would ever have thought that a freedman could rise to the position of governor?

His friend Sejanus had made it all possible, had introduced him to all the right people and recommended him personally to Tiberias. And now Sejanus was dead, executed for treason against the empire.

It was Sejanus who had taught Pilate how to hate the Jews. It was Sejanus who had whispered lies about them into Caesar's ear for all those years. But his lies had been discovered, and Sejanus had been convicted. Just a few months earlier the emperor had decreed that hostilities against the Jews would cease. Until now that had been an easy enough order to obey.

Pilate's head began to throb as he weighed all the options. He could free the Nazarene and hope that the people would not complain to Rome, hope that Tiberias had forgotten about his friendship with Sejanus. Or he could let them have their way. In a few hours it would all be over. The Jews would settle down. The *Pax Romana* would be preserved. Maybe Caiaphas was right after all and this Galilean was destined to die for the sake of the people, even for Pilate's sake.

The guard he had summoned to free Jesus and escort Him to safety filed noisily into the room. The officer asked for orders. "Take Him to the Pavement," Pilate said, walking out, not looking at Jesus.

As he arrived at the elevated mosaic pavement where judgment was announced, Pilate saw his wife's maidservant waiting to speak with him.

"Have nothing to do with this innocent man," she spoke closely into his ear so no one else could hear. "Your wife has been dreaming of Him again."

Pilate brushed her aside and took his place on the stone seat of judgment. Before he had called Him simply a man; now he shouted to the people, "Look, your king!"

He knew the effect his words would have on the people. He could have never guessed what Caiaphas's response was going to be.

"The only king we have is Caesar," Caiaphas hissed.

"Take Him," was all Pilate said.

THE BLEATING
OF THE LAMBS

JOHN
19:17–24

16b So they took Jesus, **17** who was carrying His cross by Himself. He went out to the place they call the "Place of the Skull," (which in Hebrew is called *Golgotha*). **18** There they crucified Him with two others, one on this side and one on the other, with Jesus in the middle. **19** Pilate wrote a placard and placed it on the cross. On it was written:

JESUS THE NAZARENE
THE KING OF THE JEWS

20 Many of the Jews read this placard because the place where Jesus was crucified was near the city. It was written in Hebrew, Latin, and Greek.

16b–17   The route to the scene of crucifixion always took the most public streets. Along the way Jesus collapsed. The soldiers forced Simon of Cyrene to carry the cross for Him. This was an example of Roman impressment, which said a Roman soldier could force anyone to carry a burden for one mile. Jesus had told His followers if so ordered to carry the burden an extra mile (see Matt. 5:41).

John gives us the Aramaic word for skull—*gugoloth*. The Latin word is *calvaria,* or calvary.

19   Every Gospel records, with slight variations, the sign that was posted above the cross. The one phrase they all share in common is "King of the Jews." In Matthew it's "This is Jesus, King of the Jews." Mark records it as "The King of the Jews," and Luke says it was "This is the King of the Jews."

21 The chief priests of the Jews said to Pilate, "Do not write 'The King of the Jews,' but that this One said, 'I am King of the Jews.'"

22 Pilate answered, "What I have written, I have written."

23 When the soldiers crucified Jesus, they took His clothes and divided them into four parts so that each soldier got something. But the tunic was seamless, woven from the top down.

24 They said to each other, "Let's not rip it. We'll throw dice for it to see whose it will be." This was so the Writing might be fulfilled:

> They divide My garments among them,
> And for My clothing they cast lots. 🦋

T he soldiers actually did these things.

Again and again in the narrative John reminds us that it was Preparation Day. He means for us to understand that while the Romans were crucifying Jesus, the Jews were preparing for their Passover Ceders. This involved several preparations, not the least of which was the sacrificing of their Passover lambs, which was traditionally carried out between three and six in the evening, precisely the time Jesus is covered in darkness on the cross.

---

23 The dividing of the clothes in four tells us how many soldiers were on this detail. The seamless garment was traditionally the gift of the mother to the son who was leaving home and so was a valued possession. This prize of the soldiers had been Mary's last gift to Jesus.

24 Note that John remembers the soldiers' casting lots for Jesus' garments in light of the Wisdom writings, Psalm 22. In many ways, the Old Testament contains a more detailed account of the crucifixion than the New.

THE DISCIPLE
JESUS LOVED

JOHN
19:25–27

25 His mother and her sister, Mary, the wife of Clopas, and Mary Magdalene were standing beside the cross of Jesus. **26** When Jesus saw His mother and the disciple He loved, who stood by, He said to His mother, "My dear, behold your son." **27** Then to the other disciple, "Behold your mother." And from that very hour the disciple took care of her. ❧

There has been a lot of debate as to the reason John refers to himself as the "disciple who Jesus loved." In the account of Jesus entrusting His mother to him at the foot of the cross, we see the result of this special relationship if not the explanation. John was the disciple He loved, because he was the disciple to whom Jesus entrusted the most important person of His earthly life. John simply defined himself as all Christians should, as someone Jesus loved. This is a radical redefinition of the self in light of Christ.

Pilate had shouted, "Behold, the man," and "Behold your king." Jesus' words from the cross—"Behold your son," and "Behold your mother"—tell us far more about what Jesus is really like.

She had been his responsibility, since Joseph appears to have died young. We read of Mary's presence with Jesus during His three years of ministry. We usually assume she was there as a follower, there to hear the sermons and see the signs. Rarely do we consider that she might have been there as much to be cared for as to give care to her son.

Now He is about to die, and she will be left alone. Despite His pain, despite the flood of thoughts that must have been rushing through His mind, Jesus thinks not about Himself but her.

If we did not have John's account of the crucifixion, we would have to conclude that Jesus had been completely abandoned by the Twelve. Here we read that at least one of them, John, "the disciple He loved . . . stood by." Maybe Jesus loved him because of his youth, for he was the youngest of the disciples. Jesus loved him perhaps because he was the most childlike of the Twelve. There might be a thousand reasons why Jesus loved John; of these we can only guess. What is certain is that Jesus showed John His special love for him by entrusting Mary to him for his care. When she died, before she saw His face again, the last face she would see would be John's.

THE DEATH OF GOD

JOHN
19:28–37

28 After this, knowing that everything had been completed so that the writing could be fulfilled, He said, "I'm thirsty."

29 A jar full of vinegar was sitting there. A sponge soaked full of the vinegar was wrapped around a hyssop branch. They lifted it to His lips. **30** When He took the vinegar, Jesus said, "It is accomplished." He bowed His head and dismissed His life.

31 Because it was Preparation Day, the Jews did not want the bodies to stay on the crosses. It was a great Sabbath. They asked Pilate to have their legs broken and to take them away.

32 The soldiers came and broke the legs of the first man and the other who had been crucified with him. **33** But when they came to Jesus, they saw that He was already dead, so they did not break His legs. **34** But one of the soldiers pierced His side with the point of a spear. Immediately blood and water came out. **35** The one who saw this has testified. His testimony is true. He knows he speaks the truth so that you may believe.

36 All this happened to fulfill the Scripture, "None of His

---

28 Jesus is purposely making sure that every last detail of prophesy is fulfilled before He "dismisses His spirit."

29 Wine vinegar, or soured wine, was given to the soldiers on duty. Earlier, on the way to the cross, Jesus is offered a stupefying drink by some compassionate women. This drink he refuses. The branch points to the fact that Jesus was crucified on a high cross.

35 This seems to indicate the presence of some kind of outside witness. The verse almost sounds like an intrusion of another voice into the narrative. Could it be that one of the Roman soldiers had come to faith and was part of John's community?

bones will be broken," **37** and again another Scripture that says, "They will look at the One they have pierced." 🔏

Astory *from the past . . .*
He was always there, at every gathering of the believers. Though he was now an old man, you could tell that he had once been tall. He was Roman, a Gentile like the rest of us, the only non-Jew anyone knew who could tell a story about seeing Jesus. Whenever he told it, his voice would always turn to a whisper. It was as if he were praying it as much as telling it:

"It was a cool day," he always would start out. "I awoke early that morning. I was billeted with the other soldiers in the Tower of Antonia. My company had been brought in to help keep the peace during Passover in Jerusalem. There were often riots in the city in those days.

"Four of us were assigned to carry out the crucifixions that day. The first two criminals were crying, like they always do, and protesting their innocence even as we nailed them up. Such cursing and blasphemies you have never heard in all your life.

"The third prisoner came along silently, so bloody He seemed almost dead already. Around Him was a crowd of the rabble of Jerusalem, and following close behind was a group of women who were in tears. With them was John. It was the first time I ever laid eyes on Him.

"Some time after the third man had been lifted up it got even colder, and the clouds grew black as night. For three hours it stormed all around us. If I had not been on duty, I would have gone indoors; as it was, I could not leave my post.

"When the storm subsided, only the women and John were left. The mob had all been driven away by the weather. Before, on the way to the place, when the women had offered Him a drink He had refused it. But now He said He was thirsty.

"I will never forget the sound of His voice. It startled me at first; I didn't expect to hear anything but groaning from the crosses. It was clear; I could understand every word.

"All we had was soured wine that had turned into vinegar. That was what the soldiers were given to drink in the field. We

227

found a sponge and soaked it full. We placed it on a long reed and pressed it to His lips.

"I would have thought that the drink would have relieved Him a bit, but instead, after He drank it He shouted at the top of His lungs, "It is finished." And He died, just like that.

"Later we received orders from our commanding officer to break their legs so that death would come more quickly and the bodies could be removed from the crosses. The Jews were afraid of offending anyone during their festival. Of all the tasks involved with crucifixion this was the most loathsome to me. It involved taking a mallet and striking the leg at the shin. Once the legs were broken the full weight of the body would come to bear on the shoulders and chest, and the prisoner would suffocate in a few minutes.

"I came to the first criminal and found he was breathing, so I took the mallet and broke both his legs. He never even regained consciousness. The second man was still screaming at us from time to time. I let one of the other officers take care of him.

"When we came to the third man, we thought He was already dead. He didn't seem to be breathing. Just to make sure I took a spear and sliced open His side. If He had been living, this would have caused Him to cry out.

"I saw it with my own eyes. Blood came pouring out of the wound along with the water from the heart. I had heard that the heart would sometimes burst in battle, but never had I seen the 'tears of the heart.'

"I helped the two Pharisees with the body. I spoke to His mother and the other women who were there. I met John. That was more than fifty years ago. Never, in my wildest dreams, could I have guessed that I would become one of His followers too. That I, of all people on this earth, would find forgiveness for what I did to Him."

Whenever the "old soldier," as he came to be known in the community, would share his testimony, tears would well up in his gray eyes. He would wring his hands as if he were still guilty for what he had found forgiveness for half a century earlier. John would sometimes ask him to come along on his travels as he made his way around the circuit of the seven churches. And when he would

tell his story, it was always in exactly the same words. He never expanded, never elaborated.

He died one spring while John was still writing his account of the life of Jesus. John's own death would not be far behind. The old soldier had become a great saint in our church, though he still bore himself like a great sinner. He had told the story of the cross a thousand times, never tiring of telling it to the people who would come from miles just to hear it.

The Fearless, Faithful Pharisees

John 19:38–42

38 After this Joseph of Arimathea, a secret disciple of Jesus
for fear of the Jews, asked Pilate if he might take the body of Jesus.
Pilate allowed it.

So he came and took His body.
39 Nicodemus, the one who
first came to Him at night, was carrying a mixture of myrrh and
aloes that weighed one hundred pounds.
40 They took Jesus' body
and wrapped it in linen with the spices according to Jewish burial
customs.

41 In the place where Jesus was crucified there was a garden.
In the garden was a new tomb where no one had ever been laid to
rest.
42 Because it was Preparation Day for the Jews and because
the tomb was nearby, they placed Jesus in it.

Whatever else might be said against the Pharisees—their hypocrisy, their self-righteous holiness—the only two people with the courage to go and ask Pilate for the body were Joseph and Nicodemus, two Pharisees.

---

39 The large amount of spices is explained by the tradition of making a bed of spices for the body to rest in. Nicodemus could have saved his money!

41 The detail that no one had ever been laid in the tomb indicated that it was fit to be used by a king. (We see the same detail in relation to the colt on which Jesus entered Jerusalem.)

Up until that time they had kept their faith in Jesus a secret. Whenever His name would come up in the council, they would do their best to protect Him. "Our law does not condemn someone without first hearing his testimony," Nicodemus had once said on His behalf.

The one who had first come at night and the other "secret" disciple now came "boldly" to ask Pilate for the body (see Mark 15:43). This privilege was usually reserved for the family of the condemned. Perhaps something about the two men struck Pilate as being a part of His family.

We know from the Synoptics that they used Joseph's tomb. From John we read that it was Nicodemus who brought the enormous amount of spices required to prepare the body.

What's even more striking is that it was Passover, and the last thing any Jew, much less a high-ranking Pharisee, would want to do would be to touch a dead body and be rendered unclean for days. In the passion of the moment it seems Joseph and Nicodemus forgot about their rules. They had found a task that was more important than their own personal purity.

JOHN 20

YOU WILL NOT LEAVE MY SOUL IN SHEOL,
NOR WILL YOU ALLOW YOUR HOLY
ONE TO SEE CORRUPTION.

PSALM 16:10

AN EMPTY PILE
OF GRAVECLOTHES

JOHN
20:1–10

¹ Early on Sunday morning Mary Magdalene came to the tomb. It was still dark. When she saw that the stone had been lifted away from the tomb, ² she ran to Simon Peter and the other disciple who Jesus loved. She said, "They have taken the Lord from the tomb. We don't know where they have laid Him."

³ Peter and the other disciple left to go to the tomb. ⁴ The two of them were running together, but the other disciple ran on in front more quickly than Peter and arrived at the tomb first. ⁵ He stooped down and saw the linen strips lying there, but he did not go in.

---

1   "Early" is a technical term to designate between 3 and 6 A.M.

6 Then Peter, who was following behind, arrived. He went into the tomb. He saw the linen strips lying there **7** and the sweat cloth, which had been on His head, lying separate from the linen strips. It had been folded up. **8** Then the other disciple, who had arrived at the tomb first, went in and saw and believed. **9** (As yet they did not understand from Scripture that it was necessary for Him to rise up from the dead.) **10** Then the disciples returned home. ✵

The woman making her way to the garden tomb in the dark early-morning hours is coming to anoint a dead body, not to see if the promised resurrection has taken place. From the Synoptics we know that she is carrying spices to anoint the corpse. Along the way we know she was worrying about there being someone to help her roll the stone away from the tomb. When she sees the stone already rolled away this does not appear to be some sort of clue for her that Jesus' words have come true. Upon seeing it she runs back to Peter and John, assuming that someone has taken the body, not that Jesus must have come alive again. She expects no miracle.

John again reveals his knowledge of detail that could have only come from being an eyewitness. He remembers, perhaps with a measure of pride, that he, being younger, was able to outrun Peter on the way to the garden where Jesus' tomb was. Like any careful Jewish person, John stops short of going into the tomb because, of all places, a tomb is most "unclean." But Peter, remarkably true to his character throughout the New Testament, goes straight in, oblivious to the rules.

The particular details of the condition of the tomb seem important to John, so they should be important to us. He first records that the strips of linen in which the body was wrapped were lying "in their folds." It was as if the body had evaporated through them. Later Jesus will pass through doors that are shut and barred. The cloth that had been wrapped around Jesus' face (remember the reference to the similar cloth around Lazarus' face?) was lying apart from the strips of linen. It had been folded up. The graveclothes are not in disarray. Their careful arrangement shows an absence of haste when He arose. Someone, perhaps Jesus or an angel, took the time to fold up the sweat cloth.

John tells us that when he saw the empty tomb he believed, though he still did not understand the scriptural necessity for the Resurrection. Luke tells us that Peter walked away, wondering what might have happened, still unconvinced that Jesus had risen.

GOD, THE GARDENER

JOHN
20:11–18

11 Mary had been standing outside the tomb weeping. As she wept she stooped down into the tomb **12** and saw two angels in white. One was sitting at the head and one at the feet, where the body of Jesus had been lying.

13 "Woman, why are you weeping?" they said to her.

She said, "They have taken my Lord, and I don't know where they have laid Him."

14 Having said this, she turned around and saw Jesus standing there, but she did not know it was Jesus.

15 Jesus said to her, "My dear, why are you weeping? Who are you looking for?"

Mistaking Him for the gardener, she said, "Sir, if You have carried Him away tell me where You have laid Him and I will come and take Him."

16 "Mary," Jesus said to her.

"Rabbi!" she turned to Him and said in Hebrew. (That means "teacher.")

17 "You needn't hold on to Me," Jesus said to her. "I haven't ascended to the Father yet. Go to My brothers and tell them I will ascend to My Father and your Father, to My God and your God."

---

13   Angelic questions almost always indicate that the person being addressed had no idea what was happening. (See Acts 1:11: "Why do you stand gazing up into heaven?")

18 Mary Magdalene came with the message to the disciples that she had seen the Lord and He had said these things to her. ❧

Those who contend that the New Testament is somehow "anti-woman" fail to see how central women are to the testimony of Jesus. It was a woman, Mary, who was first told of Jesus' coming. A group of women were the primary witnesses of the crucifixion. The first person to see the risen Lord, here, was Mary, while His disciples were allowed only to see the graveclothes and forced to wonder for a time. Mary has the indescribable privilege of seeing Him first.

First she is greeted by the angels. It is not as though they have just appeared but rather that they had been there all along and could only be seen now. Their question is typically angelic, for the questions of angels always indicate that the person they are speaking to is totally out of touch with what is really going on.

"Why are you crying?" they ask her. What possible reason could there be for tears of sorrow? The world has been redeemed. Jesus has risen! The only tears that make any sense are tears of joy.

Mary again betrays the fact that, even having seen the empty tomb and the discarded graveclothes, she has no expectation that Jesus is alive. As she answers the angels, she senses a presence behind her and turns around. Perhaps one of the angels looked up at Jesus' approach. She still does not recognize Him because, again, she has no expectation of seeing Him. She is in a garden; He must be the gardener.

Jesus asks the same question, "Why are you crying?" but He adds, "Who are you looking for?" The situation is emotionally charged, yet it almost causes us to smile. We are excited for what is about to happen to Mary.

Mary always leads with her heart. She makes the pathetic offer to carry the body back to the tomb if only someone will tell her where it has been laid.

She did not recognize His face but His voice. When she heard the sound of her name, she turned fully around, embracing Him, saying, "Rabbi!"

After the Resurrection Jesus will always be recognized by something other than His face. Mary hears His voice and knows it is Jesus. The disciples on the road to Emmaus walk and talk with Him for some time without knowing it is Jesus. His identity only becomes apparent to them when He breaks the bread (Luke 24:13ff).

"Do not hold on to Me," He says. These words have been interpreted in a number of ways. Some have said that Jesus, as the high priest who will offer the sacrifice of His own blood in the Tabernacle in heaven, must remain ritually clean. So He forbids Mary to touch Him. Later, however, He will ask the disciples to see His hands and feet and side, to touch Him and see that He is not a ghost (see Luke 24:39).

Jesus did not say, "Do not touch Me," but rather, "Do not hold on to Me." Some contend there has been a scribal error. By changing one letter the text could read, "Do not be afraid."

If Jesus' entire statement is taken into account, it seems more likely that He is, almost playfully, telling her that she need not try to hold on to Him, since He is not going just yet. I hear His words spoken with a smile as Mary excitedly clings to Him.

There is a note of deep satisfaction in His voice as He says to her, "Go back and tell the brothers that I will be going back up to My Father and Your Father, to My God and your God." Because of the excruciating experience He has just endured for love of them, Jesus can now say that His Father can fully be embraced as their Father. His sacrifice has made a loving son and daughter relationship with the Father possible.

FAITH AND DOUBT

JOHN
20:19–29

¹⁹ Early in the evening of that first day of the week, the doors all having been shut for fear of the Jews, Jesus came and stood in the midst of the disciples. He said, "Peace to you."

²⁰ Having said this, He showed them His hands and His side. The disciples were overjoyed to see the Lord.

²¹ Once again Jesus said to them, "Peace to you. As the Father has sent Me now I am also sending you." ²² After He said this He breathed on them and said, "Receive the Holy Spirit. ²³ If you forgive anyone's sins, they have been forgiven. If you withhold forgiveness, it will be withheld."

²⁴ Now Thomas, called Didymus, who was one of the Twelve, was not with them when Jesus came. ²⁵ When the other disciples told him they had seen the Lord, he said, "Unless I see the mark of the nails in His hands and put my finger into the place where the nails went in and put my hand into His side, I will never believe."

²⁶ Eight days later, His disciples were inside, and Thomas was with them. Jesus came, with all the doors shut, and stood in their midst. He said, "Peace to you."

---

19   This event takes place after the incident at Emmaus.

20   Note that at His first appearance to the disciples Jesus shows them His hands and side.

22   His breathing on the disciples might be a prophetic/symbolic activity (see Ezek. 37:5). This might also be some kind of partial bestowing of the Spirit before Pentecost.

23   In this verse Jesus reminds the disciples, "If the forgiveness of God is not displayed on your lives, it will not be displayed at all."

27 Then He said to Thomas, "Bring your finger over here and see My hands. Bring your hand and put it into My side. Do not be faithless but faithful."

28 Thomas answered, "My Lord and my God!"

29 "Because you have seen Me you believe?" Jesus said. "Blessed are those who believe without seeing." ❧

W hen Jesus first appears to His disciples, He does not point to His familiar face to prove it is Him but to the scars in His hands and side. He is recognized by His wounds. Before He had promised them, "After your time of grief, you will be given a joy that no one can ever take from you." This is that promised moment. The joy they experienced would be enough to carry them through a lifetime of service to Him and carry all but one of them to martyrdom.

For some reason Thomas was absent when Jesus first appeared to the disciples. When the disciples told him that they had seen the scars themselves, Thomas was adamant. "Unless I see the mark of the nails in His hands and put my finger into His side, I will never believe." For uttering these words he has been forever labeled, "doubting Thomas."

He was made to wait a whole week. Then Jesus appeared again to them. His words to Thomas might be stern, or they might be whimsical; whichever, they are not condemning. Thomas is never castigated by Jesus for not believing the unbelievable truth that He is alive again.

The Greek makes Jesus sound almost amused. "Bring your finger over here," He says. "Don't be faithless but faithful."

The one who was so insistent a week ago has now broken down. He does not put his finger in the nail prints. He does not thrust his hand into Jesus' side. He becomes a "believer" in the truest sense of the word. Thomas gasps, "My Lord and my God!"

Through the story of Thomas, John preserves the legitimacy of doubt as the partner to faith. As Pascal said, only he who doubts can truly believe. Throughout the ministry, Jesus has sought followers who have the faith to believe without seeing. Thomas, even after receiving word of the Resurrection, still insists on proof, which

Jesus gives without much complaint. Jesus pronounces a *barocha,* or blessing, on all those who will come after the Eleven who were gathered in that room. "Blessed," He said, "are those who believe without seeing."

THE MOST FRUSTRATING VERSE

JOHN
20:30–31

30 Jesus did many other signs before His disciples, which are not written down in this book. **31** But these things have been written so you might believe that Jesus is the Christ, the Son of God, and that by believing you may have life in His name. 🎋

These words sound like a conclusion. Many believe this is where John originally ended his account and that chapter 21, which vaguely refers to John's death, was written by his disciples after he died. If this indeed was John's conclusion, it was a frustratingly cruel way to leave us. In essence, he's saying, "There were many more signs Jesus did, many more interesting stories that I might have written for you to enjoy, but no."

The purpose of the book is not to be a biography of Jesus. John completely omitted His birth, childhood, and most of Jesus' life. He gave an inordinate amount of time to the last week of Jesus' life, something a respectable biographer would never do.

John's purpose is to give a testimony, not a biography. The Gospel is not meant for our enjoyment or to satisfy our curiosity but that we might believe that Jesus is the Christ and thereby have life in His name.

THE STRANGER ON THE SHORE

JOHN
21:1–14

1 After these things Jesus appeared again to the disciples at the sea of Tiberias. This is how He was manifested:

2 They were all together, Simon Peter; Thomas, the one they called Didymus; Nathanael, from Cana in Galilee; the sons of Zebedee; and two others.

3 Simon Peter said to them, "I'm going out to fish."

"We will come with you," they said to him.

They set out in the boat but during the night they caught nothing.

---

1 This kind of phraseology—"This is how He was manifested"—appears nowhere else in John's writings. This points to John's disciples as the possible writers of chapter 21.

4 Early in the morning, having already come there, Jesus stood on the shore. The disciples did not realize, however, that it was Jesus.

5 He said to them, "Children, you haven't caught any fish, have you?"

"No," they answered.

6 "Cast the net on the right side of the boat," He said, "and you will find fish."

So they cast the net but were not strong enough to draw in the huge catch of fish.

7 The disciple Jesus loved said to Peter, "It's the Lord!"

When Peter heard that it was the Lord, he tied his outer coat around himself, for he was unclothed, and threw himself into the sea. **8** But the disciples came in the boat because they were not far from shore, about one hundred yards. They had to drag in the net of fish.

9 When they reached the shore, they saw a charcoal fire with fish and bread lying on it.

10 Jesus said, "Now bring some of the fish you caught."

11 Peter went up and dragged the net, full of large fish, onto the shore. There were 153, and even though there were so many, the net did not even tear.

12 "Come, eat breakfast," Jesus said to them.

None of the disciples dared ask, "Who are You?" They knew it was the Lord.

13 Jesus came and gave them the bread and fish. **14** This was the third time He appeared to His disciples after He had been raised from the dead. 🎕

I t was the second miraculous catch of fish. Luke tells us about the first, which occurred earlier in Jesus' ministry (Luke 5:4–11). Now, after the Resurrection, Jesus caused their nets to be filled again.

ᴰ**11** There have been more than 153 guesses as to the symbolical meaning of this number. Jewish Gematria, a type of numerology, formulates it to mean

(continued on next page)

They had been out all night and had nothing to show for all their work. As they came close to land they saw a figure standing on the shore next to a small fire that had burned itself down to embers. He shouted across the lake to see if they'd had any luck; His question betrayed the fact that the nets were as empty as their stomachs.

He told them to cast over the starboard side, and when they did the boat suddenly began to lurch. The nets were full of large fish. John looked up at the Stranger on the shore. He remembered there was only one man who was able to perform this kind of miracle. He recognized the second miraculous catch because there had been a first. "It's the Lord!" he said to Peter, who grabbed the coat he had taken off earlier and dived into the water. Perhaps Peter assumed he would walk on the water to Jesus as he had before. Once he had walked, but for now it was enough to swim.

Peter made it to shore only to find a breakfast of fish and bread ready on the fire. He wondered to himself how Jesus had caught the fish. The disciples were close behind, towing the tremendous catch.

The entire incident reads like a parable. Jesus had promised them they would become fishers of men. Now, as they tow in their net full of fish, the moment takes on a significance that is hard to describe. What is symbolic and what is not? Does the exact number of the fish mean anything? What about the fact that the net didn't rip? Does this speak of divine security? It is impossible to squeeze each detail, every incident, dry. The point is that, like Jesus, their lives had become parables; they were infused with meaning. It is to this kind of life that all Christians are called. We are invited to strain and listen to what God may be telling us through the nets of fish that miraculously appear in our own lives as well as the catchless days.

The One who had multiplied the loaves and fish, who had protected them by the power of His name, who had watched over them as a Shepherd, who had washed their feet, this same Jesus had their breakfast ready and waiting. It will be the same Jesus who

---

"children of God." I prefer to see it as another example of John's detailed eyewitness knowledge. Even as in chapter 1 he could remember the exact time of day (ten o'clock) so now he remembers the exact count of the fish.

will rise from the great Messianic banquet in heaven and serve them again (see Luke 12:37). Though He is the Lord of Glory, the risen Messiah, He is still and ever the servant Lord, caring more about their needs than His own.

It is through such small considerations, the washing of the feet, the giving of a cup of cold water, that God's humility, consideration, and love are fully expressed. These small acts invite us to imitate Him. We are not required to walk on the water but only to offer a cup of it in His name, and perhaps, just like Jesus, to prepare breakfast from time to time for His hungry disciples.

A Trilogy of
New Chances

JOHN
21:15–22

15 After they had eaten, Jesus said to Simon Peter, "Simon, son of John, do you really love Me more than these?"

He said to Him, "Yes, Lord, You know how fond I am of You."

"Then feed My little lambs," He said to him.

16 For the second time He said to him, "Simon, son of John, do you love Me?"

He said, "Yes, Lord, You know that I am fond of You."

"Then shepherd My sheep," He said.

17 For the third time He said to him, "Simon, son of John, are you really so fond of Me?"

It hurt Peter that Jesus had asked this question a third time. He said to Him, "Lord, You know everything; You know how fond I am of You."

Jesus said to him, "Feed My sheep. **18** AMEN, AMEN, I say to you, when you were young, you dressed yourself and walked wherever you wanted to go. But when you are old, you will extend your hands and someone else will dress you and take you to a place you do not want to go." **19** (He said this to indicate by what kind of death He would glorify God.) Having said this, He said, "Follow Me."

20 Peter turned around and saw the disciple Jesus loved following (he was the one who leaned against his chest during supper and said, "Lord, who is going to betray You?").

21 When Peter saw him, he said to Jesus, "Lord, what about him?"

22 Jesus said to him, "If I want him to remain until I come, what is that to you? You follow Me." ❧

There is little doubt why Peter jumped in the lake and swam to the shore to meet Jesus. He had always been one of the more impetuous disciples, but his morning dip had more to do with repentance than zeal.

After breakfast and some time to dry off by the fire, Jesus asked Peter a question. Perhaps Peter had been saying once again that he loved Jesus more than the rest. Maybe he had been boasting still more about his willingness to die for Him. Peter is given three chances to reaffirm the love he had denied. At each reaffirmation Jesus reminds Peter that true love is seen in service, not merely in boastful words: "Feed My lambs." "Shepherd My sheep." "Feed My sheep."

When this exchange is over, Jesus invites Peter to take a walk with Him. When Peter looks back and sees John following, his competitive spirit still seems alive as he asks, "What about him?" Perhaps the closeness between John and Jesus had become a threat to Peter.

"That is not the point," Jesus' says. "You follow Me."

Jesus is helping Peter to find his equilibrium once more. He is not the greatest disciple. He does not love Jesus more than the rest. Neither is he the worst disciple, as his recent moral failure might lead him to believe. He is a follower, like John. What matters is who he follows.

John's Disciples, the Last Word

JOHN
21:23–25

23 Because of this a rumor spread to the brothers that this disciple [John] was not going to die. But Jesus did not tell him he would not die. He only said, "If I want him to remain until I come, what is that to you?"

24 The one who testified about all these things, the one who wrote them all down, it was this disciple. We know his testimony is true.

25 There are many other things which Jesus did, which, I think, if they were written one by one, the world would not have room to contain all the books that would be written. 🐾

One of the central motifs of the Gospel of John has been that of misunderstanding. And so now the book comes to a close with one final misconception. Jesus' rebuke to Peter was only supposed to help him focus on his own responsibility and calling. Somehow, over time, Jesus' simple statement had been twisted into a false prophecy that John would not die until Jesus returned. The writer makes it clear: That was not the intent of Jesus' words.

It seems a strange addition to the story. The best understanding for its appearance in the text is that John indeed has died. The Elder has finally gone to be with Jesus and his death has caused a stir among the circuit of churches, for which the Gospel was written.

Some say John wrote the passage and his disciples added it later. Some hold that the entire chapter was written by his followers and appended to the Gospel. How the story got there is not as important as its source, which is clearly John himself.

The second ending of the Gospel (if 20:30 is the first) sounds much like the first. Jesus said and did many other remarkable things. They might have been written down, but they were not. But if they had been, the world would not be able to contain the books that would be written. This is a positive response to a negative statement in Ecclesiastes 12:12, where Solomon moans, "Of making many books there is no end." In the light of the Coming of Jesus, nothing would be better than to fill the world with books about Him. I pray that this book will prove to be only one more.

APPENDIX

The following lists demonstrate the extent to which the authors of the Gospels used the Old Testament. They reveal the dependence each writer had upon a specific group of Old Testament texts, either the Law, the Prophets, or the Wisdom writings. These lists will make it obvious that John depends upon the Wisdom writings far more than the other Gospel writers, who base their presentation primarily on the Law and Prophets. This dependence by John on the Wisdom literature helps to explain why 92 percent of his narrative is unique.

The degree of dependence on the Old Testament for each reference on the list will be indicated by one of four markings: "V" indicates a verbatim quote from the Old Testament, and "SA" refers to a strong allusion to a passage from the Old Testament (there will be a direct reference to the verse but not a word-for-word quote). "A" indicates a simple allusion that was obviously in the writer's mind. "WA" refers to a weak allusion that is not at all definite but is still important for our purposes of understanding, in the broadest sense, the dependence each Gospel has on the Old Testament.

Old Testament Quotations in Matthew's Gospel

LAW	PROPHETS	WISDOM
4:4—Deut. 8:3 V	1:23—Isa. 7:14 V	4:6—Ps. 91:11f. V
4:7—Deut. 6:16 V	Isa. 8:10 SA	5:16—Ps. 18:28 WA
4:10—Deut. 6:13 V	2:6—Micah 5:2 V	5:25—Prov. 6:3 SA
5:21—Exod. 20:13 V	2:15—Hos. 11:1 V	6:7—Eccles. 5:2 A
5:27—Exod. 20:14 V	2:18—Jer. 31:15 V	6:34—Prov. 27:1 A
5:31—Deut. 24:1 V	3:23—Isa. 11:1 SA	8:24ff—Ps. 107:23ff WA
5:33—Lev. 19:21 V	3:3—Isa. 40:13 V	13:35—Ps. 78:2 V

Old Testament Quotations in Matthew's Gospel—*Cont'd*

LAW	PROPHETS	WISDOM
Num. 30:2 A	3:10—Jer. 45:22f	21:9—Ps. 118:26 V
Deut. 23:23 A	Ezek. 31:3ff A	21:16—Ps. 8:2 V
5:38—Exod. 21:24 V	4:15—Isa. 9:1f V	21:24—Ps. 118:22f V
Lev. 24:20 V	8:17—Isa. 53:4 V	22:44—Ps. 110:1 V
Deut. 19:21 V	9:13—Hos. 6:6 V	23:11—Job 22:29 A
5:34—Lev. 19:18 V	10:35f—Micah 7:6 V	23:29—Ps. 118:26 V
8:4—Lev. 14:4 A	11:10—Mal. 3:1 V	26:60—Ps. 35:11 A
Deut. 24:8 A	12:7—Hos. 6:6 V	27:34—Ps. 69:21 A
12:3—1 Sam. 21:6 A	12:18—Isa. 42:1ff V	27:35—Ps. 22:18 SA
12:42—1 Kings 10:1f	13:14ff—Isa. 6:9 V	27:43—Ps. 18:19 WA
WA	15:8—Isa. 29:13 V	27:46—Ps. 22:1 V
14:13ff—2 Kings 4:42f	16:4—John SA	
WA	17:10—Mal. 4:5 A	**Total 18**
15:4—Exod. 20:12 V	21:5—Zech. 9:9 V	
Deut. 5:16 V	21:13—Isa. 56:7 V	
Exod. 21:17 V	Jer. 7:11 A	
18:16—Deut. 19:15 V	21:44—Isa. 8:14 A	
19:4—Gen. 1:27 V	22:11—Zeph. 1:7f A	
19:5—Gen. 2:24 V	24:15—Dan. 9:27ff V	
19:18f—Exod. 20:12ff V	24:29—Isa. 13:10 V	
Deut. 5:16–20	26:15—Zech. 11:12 SA	
V	26:31—Zech. 13:7 V	
Lev. 19:18 V	26:56—Isa. 50:6 SA	
22:23—Exod. 3:6 V	26:63—Isa. 53:7 A	
22:37—Deut. 6:5 V	26:67—Isa. 50:6 A	
22:39—Lev. 19:18 V	Isa. 52:14 A	
23:35—2 Chron.	27:9f—Zech. 11:12f V	
24:20f A	Jer. 32:6–9 SA	
24:37—Gen. 6:9–12 A	27:12—Isa. 53:7 A	
26:11—Deut. 15:11 A		
	Total 36	
Total 33		

Old Testament Quotations in Mark's Gospel

LAW	PROPHETS	WISDOM
2:25—1 Sam. 21:1–6 A	1:2—Mal. 3:1 V	4:35ff—Ps. 107:23ff WA
6:18—Lev. 18:16 WA	1:3—Isa. 40:3 V	6:48—Job 9:8 WA
6:34—Num. 27:17 WA	1:17—Jer. 16:16 SA	11:9—Ps. 118:25f V
6:37—Num. 11:13 WA	4:12—Isa. 6:9 V	12:10f—Ps. 118:22f V
7:10—Exod. 20:12 V	7:7—Isa. 29:13 V	12:36—Ps. 110:1 V
Deut. 5:16 V	7:31—Isa. 35:4 A	14:18—Ps. 41:9 WA
Exod. 21:17 V	9:11—Mal. 4:5 SA	15:24—Ps. 22:18 A
8:1ff—2 Kings 4:42ff WA	9:13—Mal. 3:1 V	15:34—Ps. 22:1 V
10:4—Deut. 24:1 A	9:48—Isa. 66:24 V	
10:6—Gen. 1:27 V	11:2—Zech. 9:9 A	**Total 8**
10:8—Gen. 2:24 V	11:17—Isa. 56:7 V	
10:19—Exod. 20:12ff V	Jer. 7:11 V	
Deut. 5:16 V	12:1ff—Isa. 5 A	
12:26—Exod. 3:6 V	13:14—Dan. 9:27 V	
12:30—Deut. 6:4f V	13:19—Dan. 21:1 WA	
12:31—Lev. 19:18 V	13:24f—Isa. 13:10 V	
14:7—Deut. 15:11 A	14:27—Zech. 13:7 V	
	14:52—Amos 2:16	
Total 17	15:5—Isa. 53:7 WA	
	15:28—Isa. 53:12 V	
	Total 20	

Old Testament Quotations in Luke's Gospel

LAW	PROPHETS	WISDOM
2:23—Exod. 13:2ff	3:4—Isa. 40:3ff V	4:10—Ps. 91:11f V
2:24—Lev. 12:8 V	4:18—Isa. 61:1f V	8:22—Ps. 107:24ff WA
4:4—Deut. 8:3 V	7:22—Isa. 35:5 A	13:35—Ps. 118:26 V
4:8—Deut. 6:3 V	7:27—Mal. 3:1 V	14:8ff—Prov. 25:6 A
4:12—Deut. 6:16 V	8:10—Isa. 6:9 V	19:38—Ps. 118:38 V
4:25—1 Kings 17:5 A	10:18—Isa. 14:12 WA	20:17—Ps. 118:22 V
6:3—1 Sam. 21 A	11:30f—Jonah A	20:42—Ps. 110:1 V
9:10—2 Kings 4:42	11:31f—1 Kings 10:1ff	
WA	A	**Total 7**
9:54—2 Kings 1:10ff	12:49—Isa. 10:17 A	
WA	13:35—Jer. 22:5 A	
9:62—1 Kings	19:30ff—Zech. 9:9 A	
19:19ff WA	19:46—Isa. 56:7 V	
10:4—2 Kings 4:29	19:46—Jer. 7:11 V	
WA	20:9—Isa. 5 A	
10:27—Deut. 6:5 V	20:18—Isa. 8:14ff WA	
Lev. 19:18 V	22:37—Isa. 53:12 V	
11:51—2 Chron. 24:20	23:9—Isa. 53:7 WA	
A	23:30—Hos. 10:8 V	
11:51—Gen. 4 A		
17:28—Gen. 19 A	**Total 18**	
18:20—Exod. 20:12–16		
V		
Deut. 5:16 V		
20:28—Deut. 25 A		
20:27—Exod. 3:6 V		

Total 20

Old Testament Quotations in John's Gospel

LAW	PROPHETS	WISDOM
1:29—Exod. 12 WA	1:23—Isa. 40:3 V	1:1—Ps. 33:6 A
1:51—Gen. 28:10ff A	6:45—Isa. 54:13 V	1:2—Prov. 8:23ff A
3:14—Num. 21:4ff A	7:42—Micah 5:2 SA	1:4—Prov. 6:23 A
4:6—Gen. 29:2 A	12:15—Zech. 9:9 V	1:51—Prov. 30:4 A
6:14—Deut. 18:15	12:38—Isa. 53:1 V	2:17—Ps. 69:9 V
WA	12:40—Isa. 6:10 V	3:13—Prov. 30:4 A
6:31—Exod. 16:4 A	16:32—Zech. 13:7 A	4:10—Prov. 18:4 A
8:13—Deut. 19:15 A	19:37—Zech. 12:10 V	6:19ff—Job 9:8 WA
8:58—Exod. 3:14 SA		6:31—Ps. 78:24 V
12:50—Deut. 18 A	**Total 8**	6:42—Prov. 30:4 A
19:7—Lev. 24:14ff A		7:34—Prov. 1:20b V
		7:38—Prov. 18:4 WA
Total 10		8:6ff—Prov. 20:9 WA
		8:12—Prov. 6:23 V
		8:34—Prov. 5:22 A
		9:31—Prov. 15:29 WA
		10:34—Ps. 82:6 V
		12:13—Ps. 118:25f V
		12:35—Prov. 4:19 A
		13:18—Ps. 41:9 V
		14:6—Prov. 8:35, 6:23
		SA
		15:25—Ps. 35:19 V
		16:25—Ps. 78:2 A
		17:5—Prov. 8:23 A
		19:24—Ps. 22:18 V
		19:36—Ps. 34:20 V
		19:28—Ps. 69:2 SA
		Total 27